THE LEADER-MANAGER

Guidelines for Action

THE LEADER-MANAGER

Guidelines for Action

William D. Hitt

BATTELLE PRESS

Columbus • Richland

Printed in the United States of America

Library of Congress Cataloging-in-Publication Data

Hitt, William D.
　The Leader-Manager

　Bibliography: 7 p.
　Includes index.
　1. Leadership.　　2. Executives — Training of.
I. Title
HD57.7.H57　　1988　658.4'07124　　87-26973
ISBN 0-935470-40-9

Battelle Press
505 King Avenue
Columbus, Ohio 43201
Phone 614-424-6393

Dedicated to four beautiful persons —
Jennifer, Jodi, Julie, and Jill

Acknowledgments

I am indebted to many people for their help in the development of this book, but none can be held responsible for any errors or shortcomings in the end-product.

I want to thank the many managers who have participated in "The Manager as Leader" seminar during the time that I was developing the manuscript. Through their many questions, comments, and anecdotes, these managers helped me sharpen my thinking about the role of the manager as leader.

Next, I want to thank the Battelle managers who reviewed the entire manuscript and offered many constructive suggestions for strengthening the work. I am grateful to Tommy Ambrose, Sam Farmer, Bill Madia, Dick Mayer, Richard Nathan, Doug Olesen, and Ron Paul.

I want to thank my secretary, Gwen Burton, for typing the manuscript, proofing it, and getting it to publication. I also am grateful to Esther Weiss for her superb editing of the entire manuscript.

Contents

Preface

In the course of conducting management seminars, I sometimes have been asked by individual participants, "What should I do to become an effective leader?" This is a rich question. I find that the persons asking the question do not want to hear about leadership theory. They have heard enough of that. They are asking for practical advice on what actions they should take to become more effective leaders.

The Leader-Manager is written in response to this question: "What should I do to become an effective leader?" Its purpose is to provide managers with practical guidelines for becoming effective leader-managers. The book is addressed to managers at all levels — first-level, middle-level, and upper-level. And it is intended to serve either as a self-development guide for the individual reader or as a text for a leadership course.

The Leader-Manager is based on the premise that every manager has a certain amount of leadership potential and that this potential can be further developed. Assume, for example, that the entire population of managers can be represented by a bell-shaped distribution on a 10 — point leadership-effectiveness scale, with "10" being at the high end of the scale. With concerted effort over about a two-year period, I believe that an individual manager should be able to improve his or her position on this scale.

How much improvement can be expected? I do not believe that a manager who is a "1" can become a "10" or that even a "2" can become a "9." In fact, I believe that it would be very difficult for a "3" to become a "7." On the positive side, I believe that a manager who is a "4" on the scale can become a "6" . . . a "5" can become a "7" . . . a "6" can become an "8" . . . and so on. Realistically, I believe that a concerted effort can bring about at least a two-point improvement on the scale. In many cases, this two-point improvement might spell the difference between "Fair" and "Good" or between "Good" and "Excellent." Thus, I promise no miracles, but I do promise realism.

The Leader-Manager includes 10 chapters. Chapter I explores the nature of leadership. Chapter II elucidates the leader's role as a change agent. The following eight chapters then deal with the functions of leadership: creating the vision, developing the team, clarifying the values, positioning, communicating, empowering, coaching, and measuring.

The three appendices are included as an integral part of the text. Appendix A is a Leadership Assessment Inventory that is designed to help the individual manager identify his or her strengths and limitations as a leader. Appendix B is a case study calling for an application of the guidelines presented in the book. And Appendix C is a Personal Action Plan intended to serve as a roadmap for each individual reader. These three appendices may be used either by the individual manager as part of a self-development program or by the instructor as part of a course in leadership.

Putting modesty aside, I would like to view my book as the third in a trilogy. The first was the seminal book by James MacGregor Burns, *Leadership*, which provides a general theory of political leadership. The second was the more focused book by Warren Bennis and Burt Nanus, *Leaders*, which provides a theory of organizational leadership. Now the third in the series, *The Leader-Manager*, translates theory into practice.

In sum, the theme of this book is that managers can learn how to become effective leader-managers. By learning and applying known principles of leadership, managers can improve their position on the leadership-effectiveness scale. As a consequence, both they and their organizations will be more successful.

I

The Nature of Leadership

> He alone can be called a leader who responsibly leads his group—whether it is a whole people or a band of a few faithful—towards a goal that he sees. Believing vision of the goal is the first requisite, responsible leadership towards it the second.
>
> Martin Buber
> *Pointing the Way*

The Importance of Leadership • *The Need for a Useful Leadership Model* • *The Essence of Leadership* • *The Transforming Leader* • *A Functional Approach to Leadership* • *Leadership Can Be Learned*

THE IMPORTANCE OF LEADERSHIP

Leadership is often referred to as a "pivotal force." Rooted in the language of the military, the pivot is the individual on the flank of a line of soldiers on whom the rest of the line wheels. In everyday language, we may say that a pivot is a person on whom any important matter turns or depends. Indeed, the leader serves as a pivot for the enterprise as a whole, for a particular department, or for a given program.

We have read numerous times about a chief executive who was brought in to save a dying enterprise. Coming into a company that was a mere step from bankruptcy, the new CEO did what had to be done to save the company. Such replacements are not always suc-

1

cessful, but there are enough success stories reported to convince us that a single individual can have a tremendous impact on the enterprise as a whole — enough to spell the difference between success or failure.

Similarly, we have either read about or witnessed first-hand the situation in which a new leader was brought in to turn around a particular department. Perhaps productivity was down, employee morale was low, and the work simply was not getting done. But with the existing people and material resources, the new department manager was able to turn the situation around.

Further, we have seen time and again the program that was salvaged by replacing the existing program manager with a new program manager. Technical performance was below expectations, and the project was behind schedule and over budget. Again, with essentially the same human and physical resources, the new program manager was able to convert a potential disaster into a success.

In each of these cases, a single individual served as a pivot. By no means should it be assumed that the new manager played the role of the Lone Ranger by doing the work single-handedly. But the new leader did have a sufficient impact on the operation to convert potential failure into success. What was the key? The impact came about by *transforming others* — by lifting them to higher levels of performance.

It is clear that, as a pivot, the leader has a multiplier effect on the organization for which he or she is responsible. The impact of the leader is far more than incremental.

Consider a specific example of the impact of Chrysler chairman Lee Iacocca. In his autobiography he describes the emphasis he always placed on periodic formal appraisal of managers. As president of the company, he conducted a formal appraisal with each of his managers every 90 days focusing on objectives achieved, objectives not achieved, and what should be done during the next 90-day period. And he insisted that this approach be used by his direct reports with their managers, and so on down the line. As a result, his approach to performance appraisal became a norm for the entire company.

And consider an example of the impact of Doug Olesen, chief executive officer at Battelle. When talking one-on-one with Battelle managers, Dr. Olesen has two favorite questions: (1) Do you have a written plan to guide your operation over the next 12 months? and

(2) Are you actively developing a backup for your position? It is interesting to note that, after several months of such questioning, large numbers of Battelle managers began asking their direct reports the same two questions. So it goes.

As both a pivot and multiplier, the leader is especially needed in a rapidly changing environment. It has been charged that our business schools are training too many managers and not enough leaders. In a stable environment, we need managers; but in a rapidly changing environment, we need leaders. Most would agree that today we are in a rapidly changing environment and that the future promises only an acceleration of this change. Hence the great need for leadership at all levels within the organization.

For this reason, there is a need to understand the nature of leadership. What is leadership? What are the key attributes of leadership? Is the demonstration of leadership behavior bimodal or bell shaped? What is it that leaders actually do? Can leadership be learned? Answers to these questions would be of considerable value in selecting potential leaders, in educating and training managers to become effective leaders, and in laying out a self-development program for oneself. Thus, we have before us the central issue: What constitutes effective leadership?

THE NEED FOR A USEFUL LEADERSHIP MODEL

In our efforts to understand the nature of leadership, we search for a useful model. We seek some type of conceptual framework that will help us define, measure, predict, and develop leadership. Without such a model, we cannot expect to make any substantial headway in our efforts.

As a point of departure, we would like to define leadership in a clear and unambiguous manner. What is actually meant by "leadership"? Searching the dictionary for a clear definition is of little avail. Some of the definitions refer to the leading person in a group, such as the best swimmer on the team. Others focus on the political leader, the individual who leads a state or country. Still others point to the functions of leadership, such as guiding or directing an organization or group of people. Thus, we find that the dictionary merely points up the complexity of the issue; it does not provide us with a clear-cut answer to our question.

We then turn to the vast literature on the subject of leadership to seek an answer to our question: What is the essence of leadership? From a historical perspective, we find that there have been essentially four different approaches to the study of leadership: the great man theory, the trait approach, leadership styles, and situational leadership.

The great man theory has been more entertaining than enlightening. Based on the premise that we can gain an understanding of leadership by studying the biographies of great leaders, it is indeed an interesting exercise to study the lives of such leaders as Churchill, Gandhi, Lincoln, MacArthur, Patton, and others. And we do get many insights into the personalities of these individuals and how they functioned as leaders. But here is the rub: We identify both Mahatma Gandhi and General George Patton as great leaders. And indeed they were! But can you imagine two more different persons in personality, character, and style? Our obvious conclusion from this exercise is that there is no generalizable model of effective leadership.

To overcome this difficulty, some researchers believed that it would be more fruitful to identify the common traits of effective leaders. But this approach has yielded little fruit. It is a relatively simple task to list some of the salient characteristics of effective leaders: e.g., self-confidence, intelligence, vigor, persuasiveness, decisiveness, integrity, etc. But when we have completed the listing, we are left with the uneasy feeling that we have described a lifeless set of abstractions. When we select one of the great leaders, such as Abraham Lincoln, and evaluate him on our list of traits, we find that he does not fare very well on several of them. Yet it is generally agreed that Lincoln was one of our great leaders. So we are forced to question the validity of our list of leadership traits.

Going beyond the great man theory and the trait approach, the next phase in the evolution was the investigation of leadership styles. And here there have been a number of significant developments, including: McGregor's Theory X and Theory Y, Likert's Systems 1, 2, 3, and 4, and Blake's Managerial Grid. The approach of these investigators has been to identify the various leadership styles and then correlate these styles with measures of effectiveness. After some 20 or 30 years of such research, many theorists now conclude that there is no one best leadership style; it depends on the situation.

Many of the proponents of situational leadership appear to be "true believers." They are convinced that they are on the right track.

It is hard to deny that the situation itself must be given due consideration in selecting the appropriate leadership style, but a pure situational approach appears vacuous. To use this approach, for example, in developing an educational program in effective leadership, we would be hard pressed to cover all possible situations that might confront a leader. Further, this approach provides no central core that captures the essence of leadership; it is eclectic in the extreme.

Thus, we must conclude that each of these four approaches to the study of leadership is found lacking. Each one is instructive but deficient in providing us with a useful model of leadership.

It is clear that we need a generalizable model that describes what leaders actually do. Only then will we feel confident that we have a useful tool to aid us in the selection and development of potential leaders.

In addition to describing what leaders actually do, such a model must satisfy three important criteria. First, the model must define leadership in terms of *results achieved*: accomplishment of ends, results, objectives. Second, the model must deal with *how* the results were achieved because a given manager may achieve his or her agreed upon performance objectives but may disrupt the total system in a single-minded quest of the objectives. Third, the model must elucidate the *time frame* because we know from experience that some managers may achieve short-term results at the expense of long-term results.

In sum, if we had a leadership model that focused on what leaders actually do and that also encompassed these three criteria, we would indeed understand leadership.

THE ESSENCE OF LEADERSHIP

In the course of conducting management seminars, I frequently have asked the participants this question: What is the difference between management and leadership? The ensuing discussion usually is very lively. While there is no general agreement among the participants on the precise difference between management and leadership, there is general agreement that there indeed is a difference.

In their book, *Leaders*, Warren Bennis and Burt Nanus made this distinction between managers and leaders: Managers do things right while leaders do the right things. This observation may be an oversimplification but it does capture a key distinction. We have known managers who plodded along day after day doing things right but never asking if they were doing the right things. Then appearing on the scene is a new manager who indeed raises the higher level questions regarding the appropriateness of what the group is actually doing. We are inclined to view the second manager as more of a leader than the first.

We can grasp the essential distinction between management and leadership by considering two different organizational requirements: maintaining the status quo versus bringing about organizational change. If a given department is at state A and we want to maintain it at that level, we would be wise to hire a good manager. On the other hand, if the department is at state A and its survival means moving it to a higher level state, we would be wise to hire a good leader.

The essence of leadership is found in a person's ability to move an organization successfully from state A to state B, that is, to a higher level of performance. A new leader arrives on the scene, makes an assessment of what has to be done, and then does it. In carrying out this function of leadership, the new leader is able to *transform vision into significant actions.*

Bennis and Nanus provide us with a clear definition of leadership: "Leadership is what gives an organization its vision and its ability to translate the vision into reality." And here we have the essence of leadership: (1) vision and (2) the ability to translate the vision into reality. This concept gives us a cornerstone for constructing a useful model of effective leadership.

As a first step in constructing such a model, we can portray the two key dimensions of vision and the ability to implement the vision in graphic form. Viewing the two dimensions as orthogonal axes yields the figure shown as Figure 1. Here we have four types of managers as "pure types":

- **The VICTIM:** low on both Vision and Implementation, constantly complaining that the organization has "done him in."
- **The DREAMER:** high on Vision but low on Implementation.
- **The DOER:** high on Implementation but low on Vision.
- **The LEADER-MANAGER:** high on both Vision and Implementation.

This, then, is our view of the effective leader: the leader-manager, the person who is able to dream and also is able to transform the

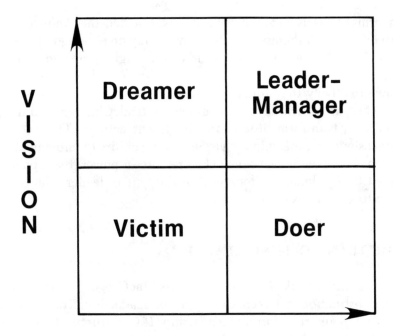

IMPLEMENTATION

Thanks to three people—Warren Bennis, Bill Madia, and Dick Mayer—for their contribution to this framework.

Figure 1. Two dimensions of leadership.

dreams into significant actions. This person is neither a mere dreamer nor a mere doer. The leader-manager is a dreamer *and* a doer. Perhaps we can best describe the effective leader as a *pragmatic idealist.*

To transform dreams into significant actions, it is essential that the leader have power. For some individuals, the notion of power may have a negative connotation. But there is nothing wrong with power *per se*; it depends on how it is used.

Effective leaders understand the nature of power and how to use it. For one thing, they know that power is found in relationships, in connections and associations between and among people. They also know that power is based on both formal relationships and informal relationships, that is, on what is given them by their formal position in the organization, as well as on what they are blessed with in terms of charisma and persuasiveness. Further, they know (if they are honest with themselves) that power may be either good or evil: good if used for good purposes and evil if sought as an end in itself. The way in which leaders make use of power will determine greatly how effectively they function as leaders.

Thus, we conclude that the essence of leadership is found in the ability to transform vision into significant actions. The two key dimensions of leadership are vision and the ability to implement the vision. To this end, the leader's chief resource is power: the capability to get things done. We look next at the type of leader who is best able to get things done.

THE TRANSFORMING LEADER

In his seminal book, *Leadership*, James MacGregor Burns makes a clear distinction between two types of leadership: transactional leadership and transforming leadership. It is instructive to consider the differences between the two.

According to Burns (and I agree), the more common type of leadership is transactional:

> The relations of most leaders and followers are trans- actional — leaders approach followers with an eye to ex- changing one thing for another: jobs for votes, or subsidies for campaign contributions. Such transactions comprise the bulk of the relationships among leaders and followers, especially in groups, legislatures, and parties. [p. 4]

Going beyond the political realm, we commonly find numerous examples of transactional leadership in organizations. Consider, for example, a typical approach to performance appraisal. The super- visor informs his or her staff that their accomplishments with regard to their performance objectives will be documented in a written per- formance appraisal at the end of the review period. The results of these evaluations will determine, or at least greatly influence, the amount of their annual pay increases. Here we see, either stated or implied, a clear transaction between the supervisor and the employee: "If you perform well, I will reward you monetarily. If you do not perform well, I will not reward you. In essence, I will reward you in proportion to your performance."

There is nothing basically wrong with this approach to performance appraisal and compensation. But if it represents the *essential relation* between the supervisor and the employee, it is indeed limited with regard to leadership effectiveness. It may achieve a modicum of performance, but it cannot be expected to produce outstanding performance. We need more than this simple transactional relation.

The better way is found in transforming leadership. Burns elucidates this second type of leadership:

> *Transforming* leadership, while more complex than transactional leadership, is more potent. The transforming leader recognizes an existing need or demand of a potential follower. But, beyond that, the transforming leader looks for potential motives in followers, seeks to satisfy higher needs, and engages the full person of the follower. . . . Woodrow Wilson called for leaders who, by boldly interpreting the nation's conscience, could lift a people out of their everyday selves. That people can be lifted *into* their better selves is the secret of transforming leadership. [p. 4, p. 462]

This, then, is the principal theme of transforming leadership: *lifting people into their better selves.* Fortunate indeed are those individuals who have worked for such leaders.

Bernard Bass describes three ways in which the transforming leader motivates followers: (1) by raising their level of consciousness; (2) by getting them to transcend their self-interests; and (3) by raising their need level on Abraham Maslow's hierarchy.

The transforming leader raises our level of consciousness by drawing our attention to the far-reaching purposes of our efforts. The familiar story of the three stonecutters is an excellent illustration of this point. Behaviorally, all three stonecutters were doing the same thing, but their perceptions of what they were doing were quite different. One was cutting stone; the second was trying to earn a decent wage; the third was *building a cathedral.*

The transforming leader gets us to transcend our self-interests by constantly focusing our attention on the mission and goals of the larger organization. We are willing to hold in abeyance or even sacrifice our self-interests for the good of the organization as a whole. Moreover, we become accustomed to thinking in terms of win-win solutions to conflicts rather than win-lose solutions. As a consequence, the entire organization functions as an organic whole.

Finally, the transforming leader helps us move up Abraham

Maslow's hierarchy of needs by recognizing our needs as individuals and striving to help meet these needs. Most readers are familiar with Maslow's well known five-tiered hierarchy, going from the bottom to the top: (1) physiological needs, (2) safety needs, (3) belongingness needs, (4) self-esteem needs, and (5) self-actualization needs. As a developmental manager, the transforming leader has an ultimate goal to help each employee move to the top of the hierarchy.

Based upon his extensive research in the area of leadership, Bass summarizes the impact of the transforming leader:

- People want to do more than they are expected to do.
- People want to meet the leader's expectations.
- People extend themselves and develop themselves further.
- People have total commitment to and belief in the organization.
- People want to emulate the leader.
- People demonstrate a higher degree of innovation.
- People achieve a higher level of performance.

These are no small achievements. The transactional leader could never expect to achieve such gains. Thus, given a choice, we will opt for the transforming leader.

A FUNCTIONAL APPROACH TO LEADERSHIP

In the course of conducting management seminars in different countries of the world, I have had the opportunity to learn about cultural differences and similarities in leadership. On the basis of this experience, I feel confident in making this assertion: There are common functions of leadership across cultures and across organizations. In fact, I would contend that the similarities are greater than the differences.

One management seminar in particular has produced enlightening results. This is an international program in management conducted annually at Battelle. With the participants representing some 10 or 12 different cultures, we have learned a great deal about cultural differences and similarities in leadership. One assignment during this three-week program has involved dividing the class into homogeneous groups by country and asking each group to describe the characteristics of the effective leader in its country. The class then meets as a total group to discuss the differences and similarities.

Some of the differences noted among cultures are striking. The Chinese (R.O.C.) place primary emphasis on two-way loyalty. The Arabs highlight "shura" (one-on-one consultation) but not group decision making. The Germans stress logic and rationality. The Swiss (from the French sector) place great emphasis on imagination and creativity. The Indonesians highlight ability to "work the system." Certainly these differences are not surprising.

But I believe that the similarities across cultures are even more striking than the differences. After discussing and sifting the similarities, we then attempted to identify the core characteristics that are common across all cultures represented in the seminar. There appear to be four core characteristics: (1) having a clear vision of what the organization (or department or group) might become; (2) the ability to communicate the vision to others; (3) the ability to motivate others to work toward the vision; and (4) the ability to "work the system" to get things done. It is generally agreed among the participants that if a person had these four attributes, he or she could "make it" as an effective leader in almost any culture.

This, then, was my starting point in attempting to identify the basic functions of leadership. Beginning with this list of core functions, I proceeded to search the relevant literature to enlarge my knowledge. And my search was not restricted to the current literature. I learned, for example, that such early writers as Lawrence Appley, and even earlier, Mary Parker Follett offer some beautiful insights into the nature of leadership. And going back some 2500 years, I have learned a considerable amount about leadership from such philosophers as Confucius, Socrates, and Plato.

This review and analysis led to the model of effective leadership shown in Figure 2. With "the Leader as Change Agent" representing the hub, the eight basic functions of leadership circle the hub and are defined as follows:

1. **Creating the Vision:** constructing a crystal-clear mental picture of what the group should become and then transmitting this vision to the minds of others.
2. **Developing the Team:** developing a team of highly qualified people who are jointly responsible for achieving the group's goals.
3. **Clarifying the Values:** identifying the organizational values and communicating these values through words and actions.

4. **Positioning:** developing an effective strategy for moving the group from its present position toward the vision.
5. **Communicating:** achieving a common understanding with others by using all modes of communication effectively.
6. **Empowering:** motivating others by raising them to their "better selves."
7. **Coaching:** helping others develop the skills needed for achieving excellence.
8. **Measuring:** identifying the critical success factors associated with the group's operation and gauging progress on the basis of these factors.

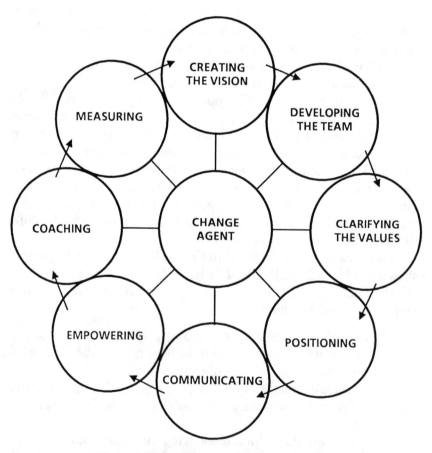

Figure 2.   The basic functions of leadership.

It is my thesis that these are the eight essential functions of leadership. While these eight functions may not account for 100 percent of the leader's job, they do indeed account for a large percentage of it. In essence, this means that a person who is effective in carrying out these eight functions is very likely to be an effective leader.

Is this a big order? Indeed it is. Even the perennial optimist will not claim that becoming an effective leader is easy. Nevertheless, we now at least have some understanding of the nature of effective leadership. Here we are focusing on what leaders *actually do.* And by focusing on the core set of functions, we will be able to take a systematic approach to the selection and development of potential leaders.

Certainly the functional approach should bear more fruit than any of its predecessors, namely, the great man theory, the trait approach, leadership styles, or situational leadership. Specifically, the functional approach should be more successful in satisfying the three criteria of effective leadership:

1. Successful accomplishment of these eight functions should *produce results*;
2. Successful accomplishment of these eight functions should achieve results in an *acceptable manner*; and
3. Successful accomplishment of these eight functions should produce both short-term *and* long-term results.

To me, the value of the functional approach to leadership appears self-evident. It is as though the cataracts had been removed from our eyes.

LEADERSHIP CAN BE LEARNED

Are leaders born or made? From the extant literature, we know that this question has been debated for decades. In all likelihood, it has been debated for centuries. In analyzing the nature of the question, we can see at least four reasons why a clear-cut answer to the question has not been forthcoming.

To begin with: leadership, traditionally, has been viewed in dichotomous terms. It has been assumed that there are only "leaders" and "non-leaders." A given individual is either one or the other. This simplistic view can be detected in everyday conversations as well as in some of the literature on leadership. Further, the matter also is oversimplified when it is assumed that leadership is a completely transferable capability. Many people apparently believe that an individual who manifests leadership ability under one set of conditions will demonstrate such ability under all conditions. This simplistic thinking has been detrimental to the development of a leadership model that would help answer the questions at hand.

Second, our efforts have been hampered by the lack of a clear definition of leadership. Does leadership refer to the best performer on a team? Does it refer only to the very top person in an organization? Or does it mean the ability to carry out such functions as guiding and directing? Obviously we cannot expect to answer the nature-nurture question without a clear definition of just what it is that we are talking about.

Third, the previous approaches to leadership have given insufficient attention to defining what leaders actually do. With the great man theory, for example, we would have to answer "no" to the question of whether we could teach someone how to become a Gandhi or a Churchill. With the trait approach, we would have to answer "probably not" to the question of whether we could teach an introverted person how to become an extroverted person. With leadership styles, we would have to answer that it would be difficult, but not impossible, to teach an autocratic leader how to become a democratic leader. Finally, with situational leadership, we would have to admit that it would be impossible to teach leaders how to cope with all possible situations with which they may be confronted. Without identifying the core functions of leadership, how can we expect to teach potential leaders how to become effective leaders?

Fourth, and finally, insufficient attention has been given to the definition of *effective* leadership. What are the criteria for assessing leadership effectiveness? Without some common agreement on these criteria, we will not know if we are on the right track or not.

The elucidation of these problem areas helps us appreciate more fully the true value of a functional approach to leadership. For almost a century, it has been demonstrated that a functional approach to *management* will bear fruit, i.e., planning, organizing, staffing, directing, and controlling. The logical next step is to take a similar approach to *leadership*.

Our approach to leadership will be guided by the following four principles:

1. **Effective leadership should be viewed in terms of a continuum.** If we view effective leadership as falling along a 10-point scale, with "10" being high and "1" being low, each one of us would fall someplace along this continuum. But it is important to note that any one of us might be, say, an "8" in one situation but only a "4" in another. Further, even in essentially the same situation at two different times, any one of us might be an "8" on one day and a "4" on another. Even with this complexity, viewing effective leadership in terms of a continuum certainly would be closer to reality than viewing it in terms of a dichotomy.

2. **Leadership should be defined in terms of what gives an organization its vision and its ability to translate that vision into reality.** (Bennis and Nanus). Thus, an effective leader is one who has a clear vision of a desired future and is able to implement the vision. Here we can contrast management and leadership. While the manager has been considered to be a person who is able to maintain the organization in a state of equilibrium, the leader is considered to be a person who is able to bring about effective change. With "Concern for Production" and "Concern for People" being established as the two key dimensions of management for the past 30 or so years, we can now advance the notion that the two key dimensions of leadership are "Vision" and "Implementation."

3. **Leadership should be delineated in terms of its basic functions.** Rather than focus of what leaders are, we should focus on what they do. An action-oriented elaboration of our definition of leadership gives us these eight functions of leadership: (1) creating the vision, (2) developing the team, (3) clarifying the values, (4) positioning, (5) communicating, (6) empowering, (7) coaching, and (8) measuring. A careful study and analysis of these eight functions will reveal that *each one can be learned.*

4. **It can be assumed that managers who are effective in carrying out the eight functions of leadership will be successful in satisfying the three basic criteria of effective leadership.** In other words, these leader-managers will achieve results, will achieve the results in an acceptable manner, and will achieve results both in the short term and the long term.

Guided by these four principles, we can now answer the question, "Are leaders born or made?" Certainly it must be acknowledged that endowment, in terms of such attributes as physical well-being and intellectual capacity, does contribute to leadership potential. But, if we assume that effective leadership is on a continuum, then we can assert that practically everyone has a *certain amount* of leadership potential. And each one of us can *develop* this leadership potential further. We can *enhance* our natural endowments. By focusing on a functional approach to leadership, we will be able to demonstrate that leadership can be learned. We should now put the polemics of the nature-nurture controversy to rest and get on with the practical task at hand of developing our future leaders.

Building on the functional model of leadership, large numbers of people could be involved in the development of our future leaders. Colleges and universities could teach leadership by presenting the functional model in a generic manner. Organizations, both public and private, could teach leadership in continuing education programs by tailoring the generic model to their particular situation. Individual managers who aspire to be effective leaders could use the functional model, either the generic or the organization-specific, to guide their own self-development activities. This three-pronged approach undoubtedly would bear fruit. Carried out on a large-scale basis, it is hard to imagine what the total impact might be.

II

The Leader as Change Agent

> There is nothing more difficult to carry out, nor more
> doubtful of success, nor more dangerous to handle, than
> to initiate a new order of things.
>
> Niccolò Machiavelli
> *The Prince*

---

*Companies in Transition • Barriers to Change • Attributes of Effective
Change Agents • How to Become an Effective Change Agent • Do What
You Can Do • The Development of Change Agents*

COMPANIES IN TRANSITION

In recent years we have seen many companies experiencing major
transitions—some to prosper, some to hold their ground, some to
merely survive, and some to fail. These transitions are precipitated
by changing external forces, changing internal forces, and the interaction between the two.

One particular company with which I am familiar well illustrates
the problems facing a company in transition. Whether we refer to
the various events that took place in a relatively short time period
as "problems" or "opportunities," we surely must agree that they were
"challenges."

The new chief executive officer of this telecommunication company had one central message in his opening remarks to his managers:
"The only thing that I can promise you is change." And indeed this

was a prophetic message. Never in the history of the company had the managers of this enterprise witnessed such drastic changes as they did during the ensuing months.

There were a number of reasons for these changes and most can be clearly identified. These were some of the causal factors: deregulation of the telecommunication industry, a changing marketplace, increasing foreign competition, mergers with other companies, off-loading of products to foreign manufacturers, and rapidly changing technology. Any one of these factors would have caused some disruption; occurring simultaneously, they brought about confusion and crisis management.

The effects of these disruptions were readily apparent. There were numerous reorganizations; there was high uncertainty and anxiety among many of the staff; and there were numerous distractions from the task at hand—namely, to continue to produce high-quality telecommunication equipment at a reasonable price. Certainly these effects had a deleterious effect on productivity.

Some two years after the president had made his prophetic promise about change, I had occasion to conduct a management seminar for a group of first-line supervisors from this company. One session of the seminar involved a panel of upper-level managers responding to questions from the seminar participants. As might be expected, many of the questions dealt with the numerous changes that had taken place during the past two years. I remember one question in particular: "When can we expect things to return to normal?" The response by a panel member was succinct and honest: "We must accept the fact that this *is* the norm." And so it goes in this day and age. Many managers will have to learn to accept this basic truism: "This *is* the norm."

To respond to changing conditions, how should managers go about the task of reorganizing their companies? During recent years I have had close contact with two different companies that underwent major reorganizations. What is striking about these two companies is the great difference in how they went about the task of reorganizing.

The first was a manufacturing company that effected a major reorganization because of a merger with another company. How management went about the reorganization would be a prime example of how it should *not* be done.

Secrecy was the name of the game. All employees knew that the merger was coming about, but very few had any reliable information about what actually was being discussed or decided upon during the lengthy negotiation period. The employees assumed that top management must be meeting secretly in a strategic "game room" laying out the master plan for the new organization. Since so little information was forthcoming through formal channels, people eagerly sought information that might be forthcoming through the grapevine. As would be expected, rumors were rampant.

Throughout the entire change process, most employees felt that they were "kept in the dark." The reasons for the reorganization were never fully explained to the staff, and what actually was transpiring during the change process was never adequately communicated. Frequently, the staff first learned about major organization changes through the local newspaper. Consequently, the staff felt that they were being treated as pawns in a very important chess game.

A major concern among the staff was that they did not know how the upcoming changes might affect them personally. Would they retain their same jobs? Would they have different jobs? Or would they even have jobs? The anxiety level of the staff was high, very high.

After the reorganization was finally announced and in place, it was clear that considerable damage had been done. Even two years after the reorganization, I do not believe that the company had fully recovered.

In sharp contrast to this first example is a company that went about the task of reorganizing in what I think is the proper manner. This also was a manufacturing company, but in this case the reorganization resulted from the company's changing its physical location.

The reasons for the change were explained fully to the staff, and the reasons made sense to them. One mode of communication that was especially effective was the chief executive's weekly meetings with small groups of employees. The employees participating in these meetings asked many questions, and the questions were answered honestly. Also, the company newsletter and special bulletins were used as effective tools to communicate all significant aspects of the change process.

Throughout the entire change process, there was no apparent decline in productivity. It was obvious to me that this was the way that change *should* be brought about.

The key difference in these two examples of companies in transition is *communication*. In the first illustration, we see secrecy, rumors, and distrust of management. In the second, we see openness, honest communication, and trust in management. Isn't the second approach just good common sense? If the answer is "yes," one wonders why it is so uncommon.

That many companies are experiencing major reorganizations, and undoubtedly will continue to experience major reorganizations in the future, calls for a new type of manager. The day when we saw the need for managers who could maintain the organization in a state of equilibrium has long passed. Companies now have a great need for managers who are change agents. They need *leader-managers*.

BARRIERS TO CHANGE

Perhaps Machiavelli was right when he said, "There is nothing more difficult to carry out, nor more doubtful of success, nor more dangerous to handle, than to initiate a new order of things." There are many barriers to effecting change. Managers who desire to be change agents must understand these barriers and be able to deal with them.

Patrick Irwin and Frank Langham highlight two key problems in dealing with change: (1) failure to accept the inevitability of change, and (2) failure to comprehend the accelerating rate of change.

With regard to the first problem, there are many managers who still assume that someday "things will return to normal." They assume that the rapid changes that their organizations are undergoing are transient phenomena. Surely these are temporary events. Eventually the organization will get back to an even keel. This is a myth!

With regard to the second problem, it is difficult for most of us to grasp the accelerating rate of change. In the past, a given high-tech product may have had an expected life of, say, 10 to 15 years. Managers planned the sequential phases of R&D, production, and commercialization accordingly. Today, however, we find that similar products have a marketable life of only five or six years. And in the future, the marketable life of these products probably will be even shorter. It is clear that, in attempting to construct a time scale for change, a log scale is more appropriate than a linear scale.

Irwin and Langham are on target in highlighting these two problem areas. But there is one impediment to change that overrides all others: *resistance to change.* This is the key barrier that managers must deal with if they are to be successful change agents.

Resistance to change is found in employees, in managers, and in the organization. There is obvious overlap in these three subdivisions, but it is instructive to consider the primary problems associated with each.

With regard to resistance to change found in employees, which includes all of us, we observe three primary impediments: habits, the comfort zone, and fear of the unknown.

Every manager should be sensitive to both the advantages and disadvantages of habit, which is an acquired mode of behavior that has become nearly or completely involuntary. Certainly everyone would agree that the conversion of many daily activities into habits serves a useful purpose. From typing to assembling to programming, employees are functioning at an automatic level ingrained by habit. If they had to "think through" each of these routine activities, they would be psychological cripples. But here is the rub: once these activities become established as habits, they are extremely difficult to alter. As the philosopher-psychologist William James noted many years ago, habits start out like cobwebs and gradually become cables.

Somewhat related to the problem of habit is the problem of employees being locked within their "comfort zones." The comfort zone is the domain of ideas with which one feels comfortable, the domain that provides psychological security. Resistance to going beyond the comfort zone is a phenomenon that is clearly in evidence in any type of work situation that requires the employee to "stretch the mind." As long as the ideas presented by the supervisor allow the employees to remain within their comfort zones, all is well. But once the ideas require the jobholders to think beyond, or outside of, their comfort zones, the resistance becomes readily apparent.

A third and related barrier is fear of the unknown. Why is it that so many people fear the unknown? Why do they assume that it will be negative rather than positive? Being able to carry out their daily activities through habit and being able to reside in their comfort zones is the security blanket that many people hold onto with a tight grip. Just the mere mention of an organizational change or a job change, for example, is enough to cause an increase in heart rate or blood pressure.

We then find other examples of resistance to change that are associated primarily with managers. Here there are at least three: vested interests, the "don't-rock-the-boat" syndrome, and being trained to be managers rather than to be leaders.

Any change agent who has ever worked with a group of managers to discuss organizational change is well aware of the problem of vested interests. Even though the organizational change promises to strengthen the organization as a whole, to the "benefit of everyone," the question that is foremost in every manager's mind is "How will it affect me?" The root problem, of course, is one of power and status. Inasmuch as an organizational change may alter the distribution of power — and ultimately status — many managers are threatened even by the suggestion that such a change may be in the offing.

And there are no small number of managers who manifest the "don't-rock-the-boat" syndrome. If things are operating fairly well, why change the system? Because of this all too common attitude, many managers reject any recommendation or proposal for altering a particular policy or procedure. The catchword is "If it's not broken, don't fix it." If these managers only knew what lurked ahead.

Related to all of this is that managers have been trained to function primarily as managers rather than as leaders. They have been trained to use the "left sides" of their brains rather than the "right sides." The exercise of the left side has taught them how to analyze, to dissect, to evaluate, to control. The exercise of the right side would have taught them how to imagine, to dream, to create visions. If managers are to function as effective change agents, both sides of their brains must be operating in high gear. Finally, we detect resistance to change in the organization as a whole. Here also there are at least three impediments: conformity to norms, systemic coherence, and rigidity of the infrastructure.

Each one of us can appreciate the value of conformity to norms. The norms of an organization tell us what is right and what is wrong, what is acceptable and what is unacceptable. They tell us "how things get done around here." Whether these norms are written or unwritten, their reality is apparent. Without such norms, no organization could be expected to function effectively. But the disadvantage of such norms is that we may adhere to them blindly, thus obstructing any change program that might threaten to alter them.

We also can appreciate the value of systemic coherence of the various elements and components of any organization. The systemic coherence is what makes a company an organization or system rather than an assemblage of unrelated elements. Here the catchword is, "The whole is greater than the sum of its parts." Surely we must accept the truisms implicit in Gestalt theory. But the problem arises when a change agent attempts to alter one element of the organization *without considering the full effects of the change on other elements.* And resistance is sure to be forthcoming.

Still a third organizational barrier is rigidity of the infrastructure. A good infrastructure is what helps the organization function as an organization. Even with excellent people, a company will never function effectively and efficiently in the absence of clearly defined systems and procedures. The problem arises, however, when people begin to view these systems and procedures as cast in concrete. To the human mind, "is" is more real than "should be." And certainly we are disheartened whenever the only reply to our suggestions for constructive change is "But this is the way we have always done it."

All of these barriers are real problems. They are endemic to any organization that is attempting to effect change. Essentially they are human problems. They reflect the attitudes of people and their resistance to change.

While these barriers are severe, they are not insurmountable. Taken one by one, they can be dealt with in a constructive manner. This is the challenge for each leader-manager: to accept resistance to change as a fact of life and to learn how to deal with it.

ATTRIBUTES OF EFFECTIVE CHANGE AGENTS

What are the key attributes of effective change agents? Or asked in another way: How do change agents differ from those who are not change agents? The recent literature on the subject of managing change offers numerous observations and insights. A review of this literature has helped me identify 10 salient characteristics of managers who are effective change agents. These characteristics are described with the source for each attribute indicated in parentheses.

To gain some insight into yourself as a change agent, evaluate yourself on each of these 10 attributes. As the Greek sages told us, "The first step to wisdom is to know thyself."

1. **Effective change agents view change as a friend. (Rosabeth Moss Kanter)**

   Many are those who view change as a threat, as an adversary to be avoided at all costs. Change means changing one's habits, going outside the comfort zone, trying to cope with the unknown, and possibly sacrificing one's vested interests. Change may mean losing control, giving up power. All of these concerns are intimidating to some. But not so with effective change agents. These persons truly view change as a friend. To them, change means challenge and opportunity. Change means new ideas, creativity, innovation, and stimulation. Change means to improve, to get better. Change means growth, self-development, and broadening of capabilities. Change means striving for higher levels of achievement. Indeed, it seems that this is what life is all about. At least, it is what the good life is all about. Yes, to some, change is a friend.

2. **Effective change agents have power tools and know how to use them. (Rosabeth Moss Kanter)**

   Change agents have three types of power tools: information, resources, and support. In terms of information, they have knowledge and expertise. Realizing that knowledge is power, change agents gain considerable influence through their intimate knowledge of both the internal and the external environment of the system that needs changing. In terms of resources, they have people, funds, materials, space, and time. And they know how to barter — how to exchange their resources for other resources that they may need. In terms of support, they have the endorsement and backing of influential persons within the larger organization. This type of support does not come easily. It is earned by establishing a track record of achievement and credibility.

3. **Effective change agents are able to deal with both the logical and the psychological aspects of change. (Irwin and Langham)**

   Observations of both successful and unsuccessful change efforts clearly point up the need to deal with both the conceptual aspects and the human aspects of change. We could very well have a beautiful conceptual model of a change program, including clearly stated assumptions, a computer-generated scenario of a desired future state, and a well-defined, step-by-step procedure for moving from the present state to the desired state. But if we have not done justice to the people problems, especially to the concerns of the people who will be affected by the change, we will surely fail. The highly rational person may exclaim, "These people problems simply are not rational!" Nevertheless, these problems are very real to the people who have them.

4. **Effective change agents are able to establish a climate for change, for rapid improvement toward excellence. (Irwin and Langham)**
   Through both their dreams and their day-to-day actions, change agents are able to establish an organizational climate that promotes change. But it is not simply change for the sake of change. Rather, it is change for rapid improvement toward excellence. It appears that the people involved are ever aware of the discrepancies between the actual and the desired, and their primary motivation is to reduce the discrepancies. Because of the confidence of the leader, the followers also have the confidence that is needed to assure that the change can be executed successfully.

5. **Effective change agents start the change process with themselves rather than with others. (Peters and Austin)**
   It is very easy to point fingers at others and suggest that they change. Much more difficult is to start the change process with ourselves. This is what effective change agents actually do. Suppose, for example, that some new system or procedure has been proposed. Effective change agents take it on themselves to test out the new system or procedure within their own units. In the process, these initiators of change acquire considerable understanding of the new system or procedure and, if it proves successful, serve as the vanguard.

6. **Effective change agents do not force change; they facilitate it. (Peters and Austin)**
   As we well know, many individuals resist any type of change. To force change on them merely exacerbates the problem. It is like pouring salt in the wound. But if the change is facilitated rather than forced, we probably will find a more receptive audience. Perhaps someone first makes a suggestion to us. Later, we are shown a demonstration and apprised of the positive benefits. Next, someone offers to help us establish a pilot pro-

gram. Finally, after witnessing the success of the pilot program, someone assists us in establishing a full-blown program. Here we can see a step-by-step facilitating approach that should prove successful, where a forcing approach very likely would have failed.

7. **Effective change agents create their own enthusiasm. (Bernard Bass)**

Effective change agents do indeed have enthusiasm. This enthusiasm "lifts others" from their lower selves to their higher selves. Through this enthusiasm, leaders are able to motivate followers toward higher levels of achievement. And our observations reveal that the enthusiasm of effective change agents is created from within themselves, not from the organization. An organization, as a collection of people, will vacillate in its moods, and this wavering will cause corresponding mood shifts in most members. But not so with effective change agents. As inner-directed personalities, these individuals are able to stay removed from the mood swings of the organization and maintain a high level of enthusiasm throughout.

8. **Effective change agents are able to let go of old ideas and experiment with alternative concepts. (George Cabot Lodge)**

At one time or another, perhaps most of us have been guilty of holding on to old ideas with such fervor that we would not even consider alternative concepts. Effective change agents are open-minded: they listen to new ideas and truly try to *understand* them. If accepting a new idea means discarding a cherished old one, so be it. The goal is to move toward higher levels of achievement.

9. **Effective change agents seek out and accept criticism of their ideas. (Lawrence Appley)**

Story has it that Albert Einstein, during the early stages of formulating the theory of relativity, actively sought out others who might find flaws in his tentative theory. This is the hallmark of a scientific attitude: seeking out and accepting criticism of one's ideas. Certainly the goal must be to develop ideas and plans that *will work*. Thus, new ideas frequently must pass considerable screening and evaluation before moving to the implementation phase. A person who possesses this attribute tends to be rather thick-skinned and does not view criticism of his or her ideas as a personal affront.

10. **Effective change agents are able to get others to "buy into" their ideas for change. (Bennis and Nanus)**
    Effective change agents are at the forefront in generating new ideas for change. Constantly aware of the discrepancies between the actual and the desired, initiators of change continually generate ideas for reducing the discrepancies. Sometimes the ideas are formulated through a team effort and sometimes solely through the cerebral activity of the individual leader. Even when an idea is generated through the latter, the effective leader is able to gain acceptance of the idea by others. The followers understand the idea, appreciate its significance, and are committed to helping the leader bring the idea to full fruition. This is a hallmark of leadership.

These, then, are 10 attributes of effective change agents. If you evaluated yourself on the 10 attributes, how did you do? If you scored high on all 10 characteristics, I say "Congratulations!" Even if you did not score yourself that well but have identified specific areas for improvement, I say "That's great!" The road ahead will be that much easier. Now the task at hand is to get busy and correct the deficiencies so that you will be on the road to becoming a more effective change agent.

HOW TO BECOME AN EFFECTIVE CHANGE AGENT

An integral part of being an effective leader-manager is to be an effective change agent. As a change agent, you need a general approach that will help you move your organizational unit to higher levels of achievement — toward excellence. Further, you need an approach that will help you bring about constructive change with a minimum of friction.

Outlined here is a general approach for becoming an effective change agent. Included are five important considerations: (1) establish your power tools, (2) develop a change strategy, (3) involve your people in the change process, (4) help your people become change agents, and (5) establish some anchors within a changing environment.

1. **Establish your power tools.**

Effective change agents have power tools and know how to use them. In Kanter's useful classification, there are three principal power tools: information, resources, and support. Each one is important.

You can enhance your information power tool by acquiring knowledge about the organization within which you work and the external environment that has an impact on the organization. Identify the critical success factors in your organization and the variables that affect these factors. Learn your job well and become knowledgeable about the workings of other departments. Also, as appropriate, learn about the marketplace. You can acquire this knowledge by reading, observing, and asking good questions. Organize the information into a meaningful framework and keep the framework current.

You can advance your resources power tool by selecting and developing good people. It is a truism that effective leaders surround themselves with good people. Perhaps you will not always be able to recruit outstanding people — because of cost and other factors. But you can select people who have *potential for growth*. Then help convert this potentiality into actuality by taking a personal interest in the development of each of your people.

Finally, you can enhance your support power tool by getting the backing and endorsement of influential persons within the organization. There are some who try to gain this support by "playing politics": by being seen with the right persons, by saying the proper things at the proper time, by capitalizing on opportunities at social functions, by being sure to laugh at the boss's jokes, etc. Others are able to gain this support through their performance: by establishing a track record based upon achievement and credibility. I recommend the latter approach. A developing manager should be aware of office politics, but to rely on this avenue as the chief vehicle for advancement is foolhardy. A wiser approach is to rely on achievement, but make certain that this achievement gets the visibility that it deserves.

2. **Develop a change strategy.**

Few managers will be successful in effecting change if they attempt to do it simply by "gut feel" or operating by the "seat of their pants." Certainly there is a need for intuition and imagination, but there also is a need for a strategy that will help a unit move from the actual to the desired in a systematic manner.

A discrepancy approach, which focuses on the differences between the actual and the desired, provides us with a systematic change strategy. It consists of these steps:

a. Achieve a clear understanding of the mission, goals, and strategies of the larger organization.
b. Formulate a detailed description of the present state of your organizational unit.
c. Create a clear vision of a desired future for your unit, and one that supports the mission, goals, and strategies of the larger organization.
d. Identify the discrepancies between the actual and the desired.
e. Develop a written plan for reducing or even eliminating the discrepancies between the actual and the desired.
f. Implement the plan.
g. Evaluate and revise as appropriate.

Experience shows that this strategy works. Experience also shows that the strategy can be learned and applied by any manager who takes the job of change agent seriously.

3. **Involve your people in the change process.**

Perhaps the most effective way to overcome resistance to change is to involve your people in the change process. When an organization is undergoing change, people resent being kept in the dark. They want to be kept informed about the change process, especially about those decisions that will affect them personally. Even better, they would like for their ideas and suggestions to be taken into consideration. Here we are dealing with the psychological aspect of change, which differs substantially from the conceptual aspect, but is equally important.

You can involve your people in the change process in a number of ways. First, you can involve them in analyzing the strengths and weaknesses of the unit. Second, you can involve them in refining and embellishing the vision that you have formulated for the unit. Third, you can involve them in developing a specific plan of action for moving from the actual toward the desired. Finally, you can involve them in implementing the plan.

The active involvement of your people in the change process should lead to a more effective change effort. We can be reasonably certain that this involvement will enhance the *quality* of the written plan that guides the change process, and we can be very certain that it will enhance the *commitment* to the plan.

4. **Help your people become change agents.**

In addition to improving your own skills as a change agent, you should help your people become change agents. A single change agent working with a group of people who think only in terms of maintaining the status quo will have great difficulty in effecting change. On the other hand, a change agent working with others who also see themselves as change agents will be able to "move mountains."

As a manager, you can do a number of things to help your people become change agents. First and foremost, through your words and actions, you can create an environment that conveys the message that change is the norm, a "way of life" for your organizational unit. Second, you can establish job requirements for each position in your unit that clearly communicate the idea that change and innovation are an integral part of each job. Third, you can establish education and training programs, either formal or informal, that will help your people learn the skills needed to become effective change agents. Finally, you can establish a reward system that provides positive reinforcement for those people who make major contributions to effecting successful change either in their jobs or in the organizational unit.

5. **Establish some anchors within a changing environment.**

We know from experience that people can learn to accept change. In fact, we know that people can even relish change if it is brought about under appropriate conditions. One appropriate condition is to establish some "anchors," some stabilizing forces, within the organization that is undergoing change.

Several years ago, a major manufacturing firm with which I am familiar was undergoing major organizational changes. The changes included new geographical locations, new customers, new products, new staff, and new job assignments for many personnel. At the apex of all of these changes, the Human Resources Department announced an alteration in the 5-point evaluation scale used in the performance appraisal program. Whereas previously a "5" was high and a "1" was low, it would now be reversed, with a "1" being high and a "5" being low. No reason was given for this change. It simply seemed in keeping with all of the other changes that were taking place.

In a rapidly changing environment, people need some anchors that provide a sense of stability. You can provide your people with these anchors. Day in and day out, communicate the organizational values, those basic beliefs that are enduring. Make certain that each employee always has an administrative "home base," a unit actively concerned about the employee's long-term career development. Maintain stability in selected elements of the infrastructure (such as the performance appraisal program and the career development program) unless there are important reasons for altering these elements. Finally, promote from within, unless the appropriate replacements simply are not available. Actions such as these will provide your people with the stabilizing forces that are sorely needed in a rapidly changing environment.

Giving attention to these five considerations for becoming an effective change agent will pay dividends. Internalizing them to the point at which they undergird your daily decisions and actions will lend wings to your efforts to become an effective leader-manager.

DO WHAT YOU CAN DO

It seems that we now have a reasonably good grasp of the essential aspects of the leader as change agent. We can learn from those organizations that have succeeded, as well as from those that have failed, in bringing about constructive change. We can understand the barriers to change, and especially resistance to change. We can grasp the attributes of effective change agents. And we can comprehend the guidelines for becoming effective change agents.

The question for each manager now becomes: What should I do? Within the framework of our leadership model, it would appear that you have four alternatives:

1. **You can be a Victim:** be overwhelmed by all of the barriers to effecting change and spend most of your time complaining about these barriers.
2. **You can be a Dreamer:** spend most of your time creating

beautiful visions of what the unit might become and then lie beside the lake reflecting on these visions.

3. **You can be a Doer:** await the guidance and instructions from others regarding what should be done.

4. **Or you can be a Leader-Manager:** create a vision of what the group can become and then implement the vision.

If you opt for the fourth alternative, there is much that you can do to effect constructive change. And there is much that you can do to bring about change *regardless of what is going on around you in the larger organization.*

Suppose, for example, that you would like to establish a productive management system within your organizational unit, a system that encompasses all of the functions of management. Following is a list of actions that could be taken by practically any line manager to establish such a system, regardless of the management system of the larger organization. (Granted it would be difficult to carry out all of these actions within an organizational environment characterized by, say, crisis management, but even here most of the actions could be accomplished.) The actions are organized according to the six functions of management: (A) establishing a philosophy of management, (B) planning, (C) organizing, (D) staffing and staff development, (E) directing and leading, and (F) evaluating and controlling.

A. Establishing a Philosophy of Management
- Formulate a set of values to guide the unit.
- Create a set of broad goals for the unit.
- Develop a set of strategies that will help the unit achieve its goals and satisfy its values.
- Integrate the values, goals, and strategies into a written philosophy of management.

B. Planning
- Study the mission, goals, and strategies of the larger organization.
- Develop a detailed description of the present state of the organizational unit.
- Create a clear vision of a desired future for the unit.
- Identify the discrepancies between the actual and the desired.

- Develop a written plan for reducing the discrepancies.
- Implement and evaluate the plan.

C. **Organizing**
   - Establish an organizational structure that will facilitate the accomplishment of the group's goals and objectives.
   - Make certain that the members of the group have a clear understanding of their job responsibilities.
   - Make certain that the members of the group have a clear understanding of their authority.
   - Make certain that there is a reasonable balance between responsibility and authority.

D. **Staffing and Staff Development**
   - Establish the knowledge and skill requirements for each position in the unit.
   - Develop and implement a systematic procedure for interviewing job candidates.
   - Establish an orientation program for new employees.
   - Provide effective training for each staff member through work assignments and coaching.
   - Take a personal interest in the career development of each member of the group.
   - Promote lifelong learning as a "way of life" for all members of the group.

E. **Directing and Leading**
   - Communicate high expectations to the group.
   - Provide staff with complete and accurate information.
   - Involve team members in those decisions that influence their work.
   - Achieve a high degree of cooperation and team spirit within the group.
   - Serve as an excellent role model for members of the group.

F. **Evaluating and Controlling**
   - Identify the critical success factors associated with the group's performance.
   - Establish an information system that will provide accurate and timely data on the status of the critical success factors.
   - Make control data available to members of the group for self-guidance and coordinated problem solving.

- Establish an effective performance appraisal program.
- Manage by walking around to find out what is going on.

I sincerely believe that practically any line manager can carry out these actions leading to the establishment of a productive management system. Such a management system should yield greater productivity for the organizational unit, and that is what management is all about. But such a transformation could not take place under the direction of a manager who is a Victim. Nor could it take place under a Dreamer. And it could not take place under a Doer. It could take place only under the direction of a Leader-Manager.

In sum, each of us can heed the wisdom offered by Tom Peters and Nancy Austin in *A Passion for Excellence*:

> Our evidence is clear. Even if the company is not an exciting one, we observe *pockets of excellence*. Excellence is what you, the supervisor (or vice president), create on *your* turf. . . . It can be done and it is done. . . . Major overall corporate transformations tend to be top-down, not bottom-up. But that is no excuse for not getting on with it among your people. [p. 322]

THE DEVELOPMENT OF CHANGE AGENTS

What will be the key role for the leader-managers of the future? What will be their most important function. In *The Change Masters*, Rosabeth Moss Kanter provides an answer:

> The individuals who will succeed and flourish in the times ahead will be masters of change: adept at reorienting their own and others' activities in untried directions to bring about higher levels of achievement. [p. 65]

Kanter's message includes three interrelated ideas. First, the leader-manager's primary goal is *to bring about higher levels of achievement*. Second, the kind of leader-managers needed to achieve this goal are individuals who are *adept at reorienting their own and others' activities in untried directions*. And third, the key role of the leader-manager is *to be a master of change*.

Where will organizations find these masters of change? It is unlikely that they will come ready-made. They will have to be developed.

We can sketch a scenario of the type of leadership development program that is needed to develop masters of change. The scenario has four components: (1) a statement of job requirements, (2) a selection process, (3) an education and training program, and (4) a reward system.

The cornerstone of an effective leadership development program would be a clear statement of job requirements for a leader-manager. A proposed statement of such requirements for a leader-manager is shown in Figure 3. It can be seen that this statement is a listing of the eight functions of leadership, all directed toward the job mission: to bring about higher levels of achievement by creating a vision of a desired future and then translating the vision into reality. This statement of job requirements can be adapted to any organization and to any level of management.

Once we have specified the job requirements, we are then in a position to develop the selection process. The goal is to select those candidates who have high potential for meeting the job requirements. Ideally, we want to minimize two types of errors: (1) selecting candidates who will not succeed as leader-managers and (2) rejecting candidates who would have succeeded as leader-managers.

We know that the best predictor of future performance is past performance. In selecting candidates for leader-manager roles, we should collect relevant information regarding each candidate's past performance. This information would be obtained from the candidates' previous supervisors (and others as appropriate). Using the list of job requirements as our guide, we would endeavor to determine how successful each candidate had been in carrying out these functions in the past. Even if a given candidate was lacking previous management experience, we would obtain information on selected factors that would serve as indicators of success as a leader-manager.

After analyzing past performance, we would conduct an in-depth interview with each candidate. Here we would have a clear model of the effective leader-manager in mind and then evaluate each candidate on the basis of the model. Those candidates who came closest to the model would be selected.

With an assessment of each candidate's past performance and an analysis and interpretation of the interviews in hand, we should be able to make a reasonable estimate of each candidate's likelihood of success as a leader-manager. We realize that we can never bat 100%

Job Mission

To bring about higher levels of achievement by
creating a vision of a desired future and then
translating the vision into reality.

Job Functions

1. *Creating a Vision:* Develops a clear mental picture of a
    desired position that supports the goals of the larger
    organization.

2. *Developing the Team:* Develops an effective team of
    people who are jointly responsible for achievement of
    group goals.

3. *Clarifying the Values:* Articulates the organization's
    values to all team members and lives these values on
    a daily basis.

4. *Positioning:* Develops a reasonable plan for moving the
    group from its present position toward the vision.

5. *Communicating:* Achieves a common understanding
    with others through effective use of all modes of
    communication.

6. *Empowering:* Effectively motivates all team members to
    want to work toward the group's goals.

7. *Coaching:* Takes an active interest in the development
    of each team member.

8. *Measuring:* Continually assesses the status of the unit
    by identifying the critical success factors and obtaining
    timely information and data on these factors.

Figure 3.   Job requirements for a leader-manager.

in this process, but we are certain that we can increase our batting average through a good selection process.

Once the candidates have been selected, attention should be given to their development. Their education and training should be a three-way responsibility involving the job incumbents, their immediate supervisors, and the Human Resources Department. The job incumbents should assume much of the responsibility for their own development through self-study. The immediate supervisors should take a personal interest in the development of each of their protégés by providing challenging job assignments and coaching. And the Human Resources Department should play a major role by providing formal education and training programs. Guided by the statement of job requirements for the leader-manager, the combined efforts of these three parties should result in transforming leadership potential into reality.

The fourth element of the proposed leadership development program is the reward system. It is a truism that we pretty much get the type of behavior that we reward. If we reward the doers who do not dream, this is the kind of behavior we are likely to get. If we reward the dreamers who do not implement, this is the kind of behavior we are likely to get. On the other hand, if we focus our rewards on those who create visions and then convert the visions into reality, then this is the kind of behavior we are likely to get.

In line with this thinking, a proposed evaluation scale for managers is shown in Figure 4. With "Level A" being at the high end of the scale and "Level E" being at the low end, the scale clearly communicates what type of behavior should receive the highest rewards. In addition to communicating the scale to all managers, the organization must be consistent in dispensing rewards accordingly. And the rewards can be more than monetary. They also can include challenging assignments, opportunities for further development, promotions, and others.

Thus, these four components comprise our proposed leadership development program. The components are interrelated and are directed toward a single goal: the development of masters of change.

In sum, we are saying that we agree with Rosabeth Moss Kanter when she says, "The individuals who will succeed and flourish in the future will be masters of change." But one must do more than merely agree with the statement. There is a need for action. And the action that is called for is for you to become "adept at reorienting your own and others' activities in untried directions to bring about higher levels of achievement."

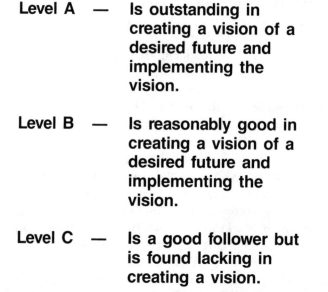

Level A — Is outstanding in creating a vision of a desired future and implementing the vision.

Level B — Is reasonably good in creating a vision of a desired future and implementing the vision.

Level C — Is a good follower but is found lacking in creating a vision.

Level D — Is a good visionary but is found lacking in implementation.

Level E — Is found lacking in both dreaming and doing.

Figure 4.   Evaluation scale for managers.

III

Creating the Vision

It seems that for the man, who does not daily dream a
while, his star will grow dark, that star by which all our
work and everyday existence will be guided.

Karl Jaspers
"Philosophical Autobiography"

---

*Setting a New Direction • The Centrality of Vision • Formulating a Clear
Vision • The Pragmatic Value of Vision • Shaping the Present for the Future
• Coping With the Activity Trap*

SETTING A NEW DIRECTION

Let us suppose that a given organization is in search of a manager
who can head up one of its departments that is in trouble. This particular department has suffered from poor leadership over the past
several years, and the results are now evident in the form of low staff
morale and low productivity. The deposed manager of this department gave little attention to staff development and no attention at
all to developing a backup. Hence the need to search outside for a
replacement.

Now let us suppose that we, as members of a selection committee, have four possible choices as a replacement for the banished
manager: a Victim, a Dreamer, a Doer, or a Leader-Manager. It is
instructive to consider the implications of each possible choice.

If we select a Victim, we will have a person who is frustrated by the system. Victims make a minimal effort to get things done and are then thrown into a tizzy by the first obstruction. They are unable to process the paper work through the system. The vendors are always late in shipping the equipment. The computer is down at the wrong time. Other managers take their best people. The Personnel Department is incapable of recruiting the people they need. Their clients won't return their phone calls. There is no secretary available to type the "rush" report. There are so many barriers! The list is unending.

Victims have a touch of paranoia. There is a hostile world out there that is trying to "do them in." Lacking the will and energy to do battle against these hostile forces, it is simply easier to resign oneself to bemoaning the sad state of affairs.

Victims who are in leadership positions have a devastating effect on the organization. Not only is their own individual productivity diminished, which is bad enough, but the productivity of those around them also is damped. This would be the worst possible choice of a replacement for the deposed manager.

If we select a Dreamer, we will have a person who has beautiful visions of what should be done but is unable to convert the visions into reality. The problem with Dreamers is that they equate dreams with reality. Dreamers present their visions in the form of detailed written plans. And plan they do. An initial step in the process is to establish a task force to develop a plan, which is followed by great hustle and bustle to do all of the work necessary for formulating the plan. Off-site retreats are essential. If clear-cut answers are not apparent, then it is necessary to collect more data, which calls for more task forces. And so the process continues as these managers pursue the never-ending task of creating a perfect plan. To meet an imposed deadline, let us assume that the plan finally is submitted to upper management and even approved.

Here we find the flaw in the Dreamer's behavior: a missing link between the plan itself and the implementation of the plan. The Dreamer simply is unable to convert the plan into significant actions. It is as though the plan were an end in itself. While the people surrounding the Dreamer may be uplifted initially by the far-reaching visions of what the unit might become, they soon become disillusioned when they realize that it has all been for naught. As members of the selection committee, we now realize that we have made a mistake.

If we select a Doer, we will have a person who can implement the visions of others but is unable to create the visions. Doers are not leaders; they are followers. There is nothing at all wrong with having good followers, but it is a mistake to put them in positions calling for leadership.

Doers typically await the instructions of others. Once these instructions are forthcoming, they will be diligent in making certain that they are carried out to the finest detail. They will be persevering in the face of all obstacles. We can count on Doers to achieve the specified objectives on schedule and within budget. Who can be critical of such accomplishments?

But the key point to be noted here is that Doers carry out "specified" objectives. They themselves do not specify the objectives. In the vernacular of Bennis and Nanus, Doers are managers who "do things right" but do not necessarily "do the right things." Once again, we realize that we have made a mistake in our selection.

Now suppose that we select a Leader-Manager to replace the unseated manager. Finally, we have a person who can create a vision and then implement it.

Leader-Managers operate with both sides of their brains. They possess imagination that enables them to create visions of things that have never been done before. They also possess logical thinking abilities that enable them to convert these visions into detailed action plans. Importantly, they are able to overcome the obstacles that stand in the way of implementing the plans. Rather than viewing the organization as an impediment, as is the case with Victims, Leader-Managers view the organization as the key resource to them in their efforts to realize their visions.

And the people all rejoice. They are now witnessing the actions of a true leader. The followers have regained their confidence because they now know where they are going and how they plan to get there. The upper-level managers realize that the department will now be able to move from the "red" to the "black" and is likely to make a substantial contribution to the organization as a whole. We on the selection committee can pat ourselves on the back for finally choosing a person who can do the job.

These brief descriptions of four types of managers as "pure types" may appear to be somewhat exaggerated. Perhaps they are, but only slightly. Experienced managers will recall having seen all four types in the real world of business enterprise.

In their study of leaders, Bennis and Nanus found that successful leaders did the same things when taking charge of their organizations. In essence, they (1) paid attention to what was going on, (2) determined what parts of the events at hand would be important for the future of the organization, (3) set a new direction, and (4) concentrated the attention of everyone in the organization on the new direction.

The fulcrum of the entire process is the setting of a new direction. This is the watershed through which all else flows.

Bennis and Nanus state it well when they say:

> If there is a spark of genius in the leadership function at all, it must lie in this transcending ability, a kind of magic, to assemble — out of all the variety of images, signals, forecasts, and alternatives — a clearly articulated vision of the future that is at once simple, easily understood, clearly desirable, and energizing. [p. 103]

THE CENTRALITY OF VISION

Lawrence Appley, author of numerous management books and past president of the American Management Association, has often stressed the importance of vision in leadership. In his book, *Management in Action*, he highlights three important leadership qualities:

> Possession of three qualities — the ability to attain a clear mental picture, to create a mental picture above and beyond what others have attained, and the capacity to transfer that to the minds of others — is a very important factor in raising some executives to high levels of achievement and recognition. This is one very important art of management, important to all managers whether they are top managers or executives down the line. [pp. 188–89]

Appley is describing a high-level leadership skill. First, it involves the ability to formulate a clear mental picture of a desired future for the organization as a whole or for a unit within the organization. Second, it involves the ability to create a vision that is superior to that which others have created. Third, it requires excellent communication skills to be able to transfer the vision to the minds of others. These three interrelated abilities are essential to leadership.

Formulating a clear vision of a desired future may be the most important leadership function. Without a clear vision, we might be satisfied that we were doing things right, but we would not know if we were doing the right things. The ability to create a clear vision is the key attribute that separates managers from leaders.

In *Managing for Excellence*, David Bradford and Allan Cohen note that the ability to establish an operative vision — to bring it into being — requires two distinctly different tasks:

> Establishing an operative overarching goal (i.e., a vision) requires two distinctly different tasks of the leader: to *formulate* an appropriate overarching goal and to *gain its acceptance* by the members. Each task requires different sets of skills. The first task demands intuitive and analytic ability to sense what would excite subordinates, even though they themselves might not be able to; the second requires inspirational and selling ability. Common to both sets of skills is an ability to think beyond the daily routine, to see a greater vision that ties day-to-day activities to significant future goals. [p. 112]

Here is the significant point: The leader is able to see a greater vision that *ties day-to-day activities to significant future goals*. Without the vision, these activities will appear to be random hustle and bustle. With a vision, there will be a guiding light — a beacon that beckons.

To fully appreciate the significance of vision, let's consider a situation in which we are choosing among three job candidates, each of whom has a different vision from the others. The job position is that of president of a large manufacturing firm, Nu-Products, Inc. Nu-Products has been in existence for 50 years and its products are sold throughout the world. During recent years, because of increasing competition and lack of leadership, the organization has fallen into difficult times. The board of trustees is now searching for an outstanding leader who can first solve the immediate problems and then lift the organization to new heights. The search committee has been actively seeking candidates for the position and, after considerable screening, has reduced to three a large number of potential candidates.

After allowing the three candidates to study the organization, the board of trustees proceeds to conduct an interview with each one. About half-way through each interview, the board asks the candidate this question: "If you were our chief executive officer, what would be your vision of a desired future for the organization?"

The board members heard three radically different responses to their question.

This is what Candidate A said:

"I have enjoyed my visit to your company and found the meetings with your people to be fruitful. The strengths and weaknesses of your operation are apparent. On the positive side, you have excellent people and a long tradition of quality products. But on the negative side, you are losing money. I have studied your financial statements in considerable detail. On the surface, it appears that you have been making about 4% net annual profit. But when you adjust these figures for inflation and consider replacement costs for your facilities, you are actually operating in a deficit position of about 4% per year. At the rate you are presently going, you will be out of business in another 10 to 12 years.

"Thus, the central theme of my vision would be *profitability*. This would be the name of the game. I would establish the entire organization on a profit-making basis. This could be done in the following way: Set up each department as a profit center and hold each department manager accountable; move more toward high-margin products and phase out the low-margin ones; spend more time marketing to the large buyers; remove all managers who are not performing; and cut out all support services that are not essential to the success of the business. Based on my preliminary analysis, I believe that this strategy would generate a 10 to 12% annual net profit, after taxes, by the end of the second year.

"What I am discussing here is the survival of your organization. Profitability is the foundation for the entire superstructure. Without a solid foundation, the superstructure will collapse.

"The beauty of this vision is that profitability will allow many other good things to happen. You will be able to provide greater job security for your people. You will have more resources that will allow you to move into new areas. You will be able to replace your outmoded equipment. You will be able to begin refurbishing your buildings. You will enhance your reputation among your customers because they will perceive you as being successful. And likewise with the general community. Thus, in a nutshell, this is my vision of a desired future for Nu-Products."

Now we hear from Candidate B:

"If I were your chief executive officer, what would be my vision of a desired future for Nu-Products? Good question. I have given some thought to it.

"I learned a great deal from my tour of your facilities and the discussions with your people. As you know, my present company has been one of your customers for the past several years. So I feel that I have a pretty good understanding of Nu-Products. I have great appreciation for the quality of your people and their commitment to high quality products. Your production capabilities are superb. The thing that I see lacking is responsiveness to customers' needs. It seems to me that many of your people are more interested in creating novel products than in responding to customers' needs. You are technology-driven rather than market-driven.

"Thus, the central theme of my vision would be *quality products for customers*. I would move Nu-Products from a technology-driven organization to a market-driven organization. One of the first things I would do would be to strengthen the marketing department. We could do such a good job of marketing that selling would be superfluous. Essentially we would stay abreast of customers' needs and then be responsive to these needs. Nu-Products could become known as a world-class organization that produced quality products in response to the needs of customers. I would consider a major part of my job to be keeping in close contact with each of our major customers. My ongoing question would be: Are we meeting our customers' needs?

"The nice thing about this vision is that it is the cornerstone for everything else. If we would place our primary attention on meeting the customers' needs, many other things would follow. Profits, for example, would not be our primary goal but would be the reward we receive for achieving our primary goal. Marketing expenses would be reduced because of the increase in repeat business. The staff should be more highly motivated as a result of seeing their ideas and efforts brought to fruition because my approach would assure that our customers actually use the products that we produce. Thus, the leitmotif of my vision for Nu-Products would be 'quality products to satisfy customers' needs'."

Finally, we hear from Candidate C:

"That's an excellent question. Yes, I have given some serious thought to the subject of vision. In fact, it is my impression, based on only a preliminary assessment, that what Nu-Products sorely needs at the present time is a clear vision of what it wants to become. This impression is based upon my reading all of the documents that you sent me and my discussions with a number of your people, including managers, engineers, manufacturing people, and support staff. Many of these people seem to be asking the same question: What is Nu-Products' vision of the future?

"It seems to me that the central theme of the vision should be *improving quality of life through new products.* This is the mission statement included in the original charter on which Nu-Products was founded. But it seems that, somewhere along the way, the organization has lost sight of this original mission statement. And what an exciting vision it is! If only it could come alive in the hearts and souls of your people.

"I have a beautiful dream for your organization! Nu-Products could become a recognized world leader in improving quality of life through the development of new products. Just think of all the people in the world who have a crying need to improve their quality of life. And what tremendous resources you have to bring to bear on this need. I believe that Nu-Products has the potential for being the world's leading organization that is directing its efforts toward this single goal: improving quality of life for the people of the world through new products.

"I believe that if you would direct your energies toward this single overarching goal, then other things would fall in place. Certainly such a vision would be uplifting to all of your staff, which would mean that they would work harder and be more productive . . . which would mean that you would better meet the needs of your customers . . . which means that you would be financially profitable. I would like very much to help Nu-Products convert this vision into reality."

This was the gist of the three responses given to what the board members considered to be their most penetrating question. After the third interview was completed, the members convened to decide which of the three candidates would be their new chief executive officer.

A difficult decision? Indeed it is. If you were a member of the board of trustees, which candidate would you choose? Because you have been provided with only limited information on Nu-Products and the three candidates, this may be an impossible question to answer. But even so, it is important to appreciate that there is no "right" answer.

The point to be made is that, regardless of which candidate is chosen, the candidate's vision for the future of the organization will have a *profound impact on the organization.* To a somewhat lesser extent, the same holds true for managers down the line. The manager's vision is central to the direction and the ultimate success of the organization.

FORMULATING A CLEAR VISION

We need to address two questions: (1) What is meant by a "vision"? and (2) How does one go about creating a vision?

With regard to the first question, Bennis and Nanus elucidate the nature of a vision:

> To choose a direction, a leader must first have developed a mental image of a possible and desirable future state of the organization. This image, which we call a *vision,* may be as vague as a dream or as precise as a goal or mission statement. The critical point is that a vision articulates a view of a realistic, credible, attractive future for the organization, a condition that is better in some important ways than what now exists. [p. 89]

With regard to the second question, I would like to tell a relevant anecdote. The setting was an international seminar on R&D management that I was directing. We had as participants some 25 middle-level R&D managers from a number of different countries. The speaker for the session on Effective Leadership was Doug Olesen, a senior manager at Battelle.

In his description of key characteristics of effective leaders, Doug made special note of the leader's ability to create a clear vision to guide the unit. At this point in the presentation, Doug was interrupted by one of the participants. It seemed apparent from the tone of voice and body language that this participant accepted the importance of vision, but he wanted to know exactly how a manager should go about creating the vision.

The question was phrased in these words: "I understand what you are saying about the importance of vision. But what I want to know is how you go about creating the vision. Are you lying on the beach basking in the sun when all of a sudden you exclaim, 'Eureka! I have the vision!'?"

After a bit of friendly chuckling from the other participants, Doug responded that the creation of a vision was not that simple. It required a great deal of hard work. Further, he noted that the vision did not emerge spontaneously but came into being through a systematic process.

Indeed, the vision is developed through a systematic process. Below I have outlined a procedure for developing a vision. The procedure consists of eight steps:

1. **Study the mission, goals, and strategic plans of the larger organization.** Make certain that you have a clear understanding of the organization's central mission — its reason for existence. Also, make certain that you have a clear understanding of the broad goals that support this mission. Study the organization's strategic plan in depth, including major thrust areas, priorities, any planned changes in direction, and new skills that might be required. Make special note of how your unit might contribute to the strategic plan.

2. **Analyze your organizational unit.** Study the past, present, and future of the unit. With regard to the past, what have been the significant experiences and learning that can contribute to the future? With regard to the present, what are the unit's strengths and weaknesses? With regard to the future, what do you anticipate will be the demand for the unit's products or services?

3. **Draft a preliminary statement of vision.** Develop a first draft of a desired future state for your organizational unit. Include a description of mission, major thrust areas, the type of organizational structure, and the type of people. Also include how you expect to be viewed by your clients.

4. **Review the draft with others.** Important here will be to review the preliminary description of vision with your manager. Also important will be to review the description with your people. Actively seek their comments and recommendations. Be a good listener.

5. **Revise the preliminary statement of vision as appropriate.** You should have taken good notes when reviewing the preliminary statement of vision with your manager and your

people. Reflect on these notes. Then use this information to embellish and strengthen the statement of vision. At this point it would be appropriate to get the revised version typed and distributed to all of the interested parties.

6. **Incorporate the vision in the unit's plans and systems.** For the vision to become a reality, it must be incorporated in the unit's operational plan and systems. Include the vision as the leitmotif of the unit's annual plan. Establish an organizational structure that supports the vision. Develop a staffing and staff development program that supports the vision. Tailor the performance appraisal program so that it supports the vision. Develop a reward system that reinforces those behaviors that lead toward the vision.

7. **Measure progress of the unit in the light of the vision.** Identify the critical success factors associated with the vision. Make certain that you are receiving timely data on the status of each of these factors. Then measure your progress on the basis of how well the unit is performing on each of these factors.

8. **Periodically evaluate the vision for possible modifications.** You cannot expect to cast the vision in concrete. The external environment changes. The internal environment changes. And the interaction between the external environment and the internal environment changes. Further, you may not have been quite on target with the initial vision. In the light of these considerations, it is essential that you periodically evaluate the vision for possible realignments.

As can be seen, we are describing here a process for both creating the vision *and* implementing the vision. Creating the vision without implementing it is a futile exercise. Trying to implement without having a clear vision is a blind exercise. Combining the two can result in a significant transformation of the unit.

Carrying out this process requires some special skills on the part of the manager. Especially noteworthy are two skills: the ability to ask good questions and the ability to listen.

These two skills are highlighted by Bennis and Nanus:

> The leader must be a superb listener, particularly to those advocating new or different images of the emerging reality. Many leaders establish both formal and informal channels

of communication to gain access to these ideas. Most leaders
also spend a substantial portion of their time interacting
with advisers, consultants, other leaders, scholars, planners,
and a wide variety of other people both inside and outside
their own organizations in this search. Successful leaders,
we have found, are *great askers*, and they do pay attention. [p. 96]

THE PRAGMATIC VALUE OF VISION

A hard-nosed pragmatist may have difficulty appreciating the value
of a clear vision. Visions smack of dreams. Dreams are not made
of the same stuff as the basic ingredients of a successful enterprise —
hard work, efficiency, productivity, market share, and bottom-line
profits. But vision indeed has pragmatic value. It is the key agent
for all of the other ingredients.

Bennis and Nanus put the matter in perspective:

> When the organization has a clear sense of its purpose,
> direction, and desired future state, and when this image
> is widely shared, individuals are able to find their own roles
> both in the organization and in the larger society of which
> they are a part. This empowers individuals and confers
> status upon them because they can see themselves as part
> of a worthwhile enterprise. They gain a sense of impor-
> tance, as they are transformed from robots blindly follow-
> ing instructions to human beings engaged in a creative and
> purposeful venture. [pp. 90–91]

In a pragmatic sense, the presence of a clear vision offers a number
of distinct benefits to the organization as a whole as well as to all
of the people in the organization. For the manager, a clear vision
aids considerably in carrying out each of the basic functions of
management. Included here are planning, organizing, staffing and
staff development, directing and leading, and evaluating and
controlling.

1. **A clear vision aids in planning.**
    Planning involves developing a roadmap for getting from A
    to B, from the present to the future. It is important to note that
    a good plan is not merely a forecast of what is *likely* to happen;
    it is a roadmap of what the planners want to *make* happen.

I recall meeting with a new manager of a section in an engineering consulting firm to discuss his plans for a one-day retreat. The purpose of the retreat was to involve his senior-level people in developing an operational plan for the coming year. He had asked me to meet with him to review the tentative agenda that he had prepared for the coming event. Included in the agenda were these items: review of strengths and weaknesses of the section, discussion of market opportunities, specification of technical thrust areas, identification of staffing needs, identification of equipment needs, and formulation of budget. This was all fine and good, but the one important item that was missing from the agenda was a delineation of the vision for the future of the section. After we talked over this matter in some detail, he agreed that a discussion of vision should be included in the day's agenda.

This young manager informed me later that he did indeed present to the group his vision for the section, which generated considerable discussion. He said that the beauty of the vision was that it served as the integrating theme for the day — as well as for the subsequently developed written plan.

2. A clear vision aids in organizing.

Organizing involves arranging all of the key activities of the enterprise (or unit) into a coherent whole. In practically every type of enterprise, there is a need for an organizational structure that clarifies job functions, responsibilities, and reporting relationships.

Far too often managers make organization-type decisions purely on the basis of the needs of the day. And this short-term approach continues over an extended period of time. Then, on a given day, the manager looks at the organizational structure and asks, "How did we ever arrive at *this* organizational structure?" It was arrived at by a series of discrete decisions that were made along the way without any consideration given to what the future organizational structure should look like. It would be far more effective if each manager would carry two organizational structures in his or her head: the present one and a desired future one that supports the vision. Then, as organization-type decisions are required along the way, they should be made *in the light of the desired future organizational structure.*

3. **A clear vision aids in staffing and staff development.**

Staffing and staff development involve recruiting the people and then developing them into an effective working group. Without competent people who are well qualified to carry out their job functions, no enterprise can be expected to succeed.

What kind of people do we need? When do you need them? These are basic human resources questions that every manager must answer. Again, far too often the questions are answered on an "as needed" basis. "Joe needs a programmer, so let's contact Personnel." "Mary Lou needs an analyst, so let's contact Personnel." "Pete wants to take the course in Computer Graphics. Can our budget cover it?" And so it goes. Each decision is made on an ad hoc basis, to meet an immediate need, without any clear notion of the type of human resources capabilities that will be needed in the future. A far more effective approach would be to make the decisions *in the light of the overall human resources capabilities desired for the future.*

4. **A clear vision aids in directing and leading.**

To assure an effective and efficient operation, there are a number of activities that the manager must carry out on a day-to-day basis. Even though the manager may have done an excellent job in planning, organizing, and staffing and staff development, there is still the need to give special attention to directing and leading on an ongoing basis. Here there are two particularly important activities: communicating and motivating.

With regard to meeting the communication needs of their employees, managers should be sensitive to the fact that most employees want answers to some fairly basic questions: Where are we going? How do we plan to get there? What role do you expect me to play? How will my job change? If satisfactory answers are not forthcoming, the employees will be uneasy, to say the least. Think what a difference it would make if the unit manager would hold up a clear vision of the desired future for the unit and then continually communicate this vision in both words and actions. This single activity alone would meet a significant portion of the staff's communication needs.

Communicating the vision also is likely to have a positive impact on employee motivation. Without vision, employees are limited to the world of empirical existence: Their efforts are directed toward simply "earning a living." With a clear vision, employees are able to transcend their mere empirical existence because their lives are infused with meaning. Here we should be reminded of the words of Nietzsche when he says, "He who has a *why* to live for can bear almost any *how*."

5. **A clear vision aids in evaluating and controlling.**

Evaluating and controlling involve making sure that the plans succeed. Carrying out this function includes establishing standards against which performance can be measured, measuring performance, and correcting deviations from the standards or plans. In essence, this means that you first must determine whether or not you are on the right track, and if you are not, then do whatever is necessary to get back on track.

Most managers spend a substantial portion of their time evaluating and controlling their operations. This function often is carried out within a short-term time perspective. What is heard most frequently throughout the offices, conference rooms, and corridors is this question: "How did we do this month?" By focusing only on short-term results, managers may conclude that they are doing things *right*, but they may not really know if they are doing the *right things*. They may very well lose sight of their long-term goals, their vision.

The existence of a clear vision helps the manager focus on the essentials. Foremost in every manager's mind should be this question: Are our current decisions and results moving us toward the vision or away from the vision? With this approach, the evaluating and controlling function is carried out *in the light of the vision*.

Indeed, it should be apparent that a clear vision has pragmatic value for the organization as a whole, as well as for every manager in the organization. The vision can serve as the key agent in guiding the entire array of management functions.

Without a clear vision, a manager would be like an artist who begins a painting without any clear notion of what is to be painted. Such a trial-and-error approach might perchance turn out well, but the odds are against it.

SHAPING THE PRESENT FOR THE FUTURE

Of the hundreds of management books that have been published during this century, a few stand out as true classics. One such classic is Chester Barnard's *Organization and Management*. There is much wisdom in this book, but especially significant is this message: *Managers should shape the present for the future.*

> It is the nature of a leader's work that he should be a realist and should recognize the need for action, even when the outcome cannot be foreseen, but also that he should be an idealist and in the broadest sense pursue goals some of which can only be attained in a succeeding generation of leaders. . . . To neglect today for tomorrow surely reflects a treacherous sentimentalism; but to shape the present for the future by the surplus of thought and purpose which we now can muster seems the very expression of the idealism which underlies such social coherence as we presently achieve, and without this idealism we see no worthy meaning in our lives, our institutions, or our culture. [p. 100]

In this view of a leader's work, Barnard makes several salient points:

1. **The leader should be a realist and should recognize the need for action.** The leader cannot be a mere dreamer. Nor can the leader be a mere observer of an interesting scene. It is essential that the leader reside in the world of empirical existence, the world of problems, deadlines, limited resources, conflicts, challenges, frustrations, successes, and failures.

2. **The leader also should be an idealist and pursue some far-reaching goals.** As an idealist, the leader can transcend the world of empirical existence and devote some of his or her time to dreaming, contemplating far-reaching goals that go far beyond that which now exists. The world of imagination and dreams is not made of the same stuff as that of the world of empirical existence, but it is just as vital to the leadership function.

3. **To neglect today for tomorrow surely reflects a treacherous sentimentalism.** Indeed, it is as though the leader must wear bifocal glasses, with the lower half of the lens directed toward the needs of the day and the upper half directed toward the dreams for the future. Both halves of the lens are essential.

4. **The leader should shape the present for the future.** Effective leaders are able to gaze through both halves of the bifocal lens simultaneously. They do this by immersing themselves

in the decisions of the day and *concurrently* directing these decisions toward the vision of a desired future.

Shaping the present for the future is incrementalism at its best. While creating the initial vision may have come about through a magnificent leap, moving the unit from the present situation toward the vision requires a different tack. As indicated in Figure 5, we are looking here at a series of discrete decisions, each of which may have only a minor impact but collectively can alter the course substantially.

To illustrate the point, let's consider how two different department managers might approach some of the typical decisions they must make on a day-to-day basis. Manager A is oriented toward "staying the course"; Manager B is oriented toward "shaping the present for the future." Try to put yourself in the place of each of these two managers and reflect on how you would approach each decision.

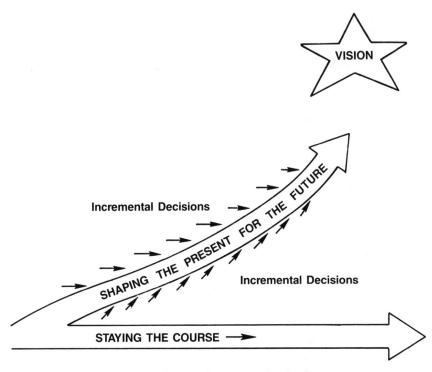

Figure 5. Shaping the present for the future.

Planning
- Deciding on the goals and objectives of the group for the coming year.
- Deciding on thrust areas for the coming year
- Deciding on priorities for the coming year
- Deciding on which clients to cultivate
- Deciding on which personal computers to buy for the group
- Deciding on which computer software to purchase
- Deciding on budget allocations for the year

Organizing
- Deciding on an appropriate organizational structure
- Deciding on what job tasks to delegate to others and to whom

Staffing and Staff Development
- Deciding on which job candidate to select for a given job position
- Deciding on which staff education and training programs to support
- Deciding on what types of departmental seminars to support
- Deciding on which professional meetings to attend
- Deciding on which individuals to promote to key positions in the department

Directing and Leading
- Deciding on what to include in monthly staff meetings
- Deciding on what types of staff behavior to reinforce
- Deciding on the priorities of various problems that must be solved

Evaluating and Controlling
- Deciding on what data to store in the management information system
- Deciding on what equipment to phase out, what to "write off"
- Deciding on how much annual net profit to show for the department

You probably will agree that many of these are typical decisions facing many department managers. You also probably will agree that Manager A and Manager B would respond quite differently to each of these situations. Essentially, Manager A would make each decision in such a manner that it would help stay the course. Manager B, on the other hand, would make each decision *in the light of the vision*.

Another point to appreciate is that each of these decisions is *incremental*: It is one small additional step that should help move the department in the desired direction. As stressed by Peters and Waterman, excellence does not come about through one grand and magnificent action. It comes about by doing a whole bunch of little things in an excellent manner.

In sum, the message from Chester Barnard is that the manager should shape the present for the future. The task will not be easy. You will be faced with many obstacles, primarily in the form of pressures to devote your total self to the immediate problems at hand. But if you are able to overcome these obstacles by keeping your eyes focused on the vision while still coping with day-to-day problems, then surely you are likely to make considerable progress in moving toward the far-reaching vision. We should be reminded constantly of Chester Barnard's admonition: "Without this idealism we see no worthy meaning in our lives, our institutions, or our culture."

COPING WITH THE ACTIVITY TRAP

Many people get so caught up in their activities that they lose sight of the vision. It is as though activities are the only reality, and the vision is merely an abstraction, something akin to Plato's eternal ideas.

In the course of conducting a Principles of Management seminar for managers in many different organizations and a number of different cultures, I have become acutely aware of the problem of the Activity Trap. In a session on time management, I ask the participants to relate their activities to their goals. The step involving the listing of activities and the amount of time devoted to each is fairly straightforward. But then when I ask the participants to state the overarching goal of their units, there often is a period of silence. Taking a different tack, I ask them to state the primary mission of their units — and there is still a period of silence. Then finally, I will ask, "Why is your department in business? What is its reason for existence?" And here I will begin to get some answers, but only after considerable persistence.

From this experience, it has become clear to me that many managers give their primary attention to their day-to-day activities *without any clear notion of what overarching goal these activities are directed toward.* These managers are absorbed in the *how* of their work without any clear understanding of the *why.* If these were robots we are talking about, there would be no reason for concern. But these are mature human beings, individuals who are charged with managing the work of others.

George Odiorne, the well known expert on management by objectives, has given considerable attention to the enigma of the Activity Trap. In his book, *MBO II,* he highlights these problems:

1. People get so enmeshed in activity that they lose sight of the purpose of their work.
2. People caught in the Activity Trap diminish in capability rather than grow.
3. The Activity Trap originates at the top of organizations and extends to the lowest levels.
4. Organizations that have become Activity Traps kill motivation of people working in them.
5. Most problems don't get solved in activity-centered organizations, and some problems get worse.
6. Activity-centered managers avoid reality by converting it into something else.

Getting caught up in the Activity Trap has serious implications, all of which lessen one's own productivity as well as the productivity of the organization as a whole. Here are some of the obvious implications:

1. Primary attention is given to "doing things right" rather than "doing the right things."
2. There is lack of useful framework for establishing priorities and sorting out activities.
3. Long-term goals are given a back seat (or no seat at all) to immediate activities.
4. Little thought is given to innovation and how to do things better, to reduce the gap between the "is" and the "should be."
5. The problem is simply exacerbated when managers attempt to work harder rather than work smarter.

Is there a way out of the Activity Trap? I think there is. The specialists in time management have provided us with a procedure for escaping the tentacles of the Activity Trap. It is a straightforward exercise consisting of the following steps.

First, formulate a clear statement of the overarching goal of your unit (section, department, or company). This is the overall mission of your unit, its reason for existence. The statement of overarching goal should be written in terms of your primary products or services that are designed to meet customer needs.

Second, write your three to five key performance objectives for the year. These are the ends or aims toward which your activities should be directed. Reflect on how these performance objectives contribute to the overarching goal.

Third, systematically record how you spend your time in a given week. In 15-minute increments, keep a tally of your activities each day. At the end of the week, list all of the activities and how much time was devoted to each.

Fourth, align the activities with the objectives. With a clean table or desk and a pack of 3×5 cards, this step will take about one hour. Write the overarching goal, the performance objectives, and the activities (with the associated times) on individual 3×5 cards. Then, using Figure 6 as a guide, lay out the cards as indicated.

This step may reveal some surprising results. You may find that one or more of your objectives have no activity cards beneath them. You may find that you have a number of activity cards that are not related to any of your performance objectives. Or you may discover that the time allotments associated with certain activities are not consistent with the relative importance of the objectives that these activities support. Any of these findings should give you reason to ponder over how you are spending your time.

Fifth, develop a plan of action for improving your time management. Identify the barriers and determine how you will overcome the barriers. Develop specific action steps that can be taken immediately.

Sixth, and finally, implement the plan of action. And do not be disheartened if you are not successful in implementing all aspects of your plan immediately. It is important to realize that you are dealing with well-ingrained habits and behaviors, many of which may take some time to modify. And be sure to pat yourself on the back for your successes.

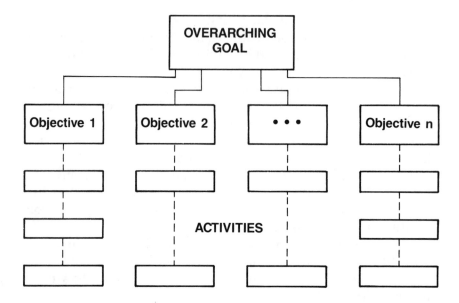

Figure 6.   Aligning activities with objectives.

If you have never gone through this exercise, I believe that you will find it worthwhile. You may find it useful to go through it at least once each year.

In sum, our message is simple and straightforward: Every manager should be aware of the Activity Trap. As a manager, you have a twofold responsibility: (1) to manage your own time well and (2) to help your people manage their time well.

You and each of your people should be able to answer this question:

> WHAT IS THE OVERARCHING GOAL OF
> MY UNIT AND HOW ARE MY ACTIVITIES
> RELATED TO THIS GOAL?

IV

Developing the Team

Fail to honor people
They fail to honor you;
But of a good leader, who talks little,
When his work is done, his aim fulfilled,
They will all say, "We did this ourselves."

Lao Tzu
Book of Tao

Limitations of Heroic Managers • The Changing Role of the Manager •
The Need for Team Leaders • The Productive Team • Developing a Pro-
ductive Team • Benefits of a Team Approach

LIMITATIONS OF HEROIC MANAGERS

In *Managing for Excellence*, David Bradford and Allan Cohen give
us a vivid description of the heroic manager:

> When American managers talk about their vision of man-
> aging—the idealized models of their imagination—the
> same few cultural heroes glorified in film and fiction are
> frequently mentioned. Heroic managers secretly view them-
> selves as direct descendents of the frontiersman, that quiet
> but tough adventurer who was constantly setting out for
> new territory, long an ideal in American literature, film,
> mythology, and consciousness. The Lone Ranger, an im-
> posing masked figure, rides up on a white horse to over-

> come great odds in solving the problem of the day. This model of the vanquishing leader—a bit mysterious, generous but aloof—is a very common theme. [p. 26]

The two authors then go on to stress that the most paradoxical and frustrating trap for the heroic manager is that greater effort "exacerbates the problem." While increasingly greater efforts are demanded of the leader, the abilities and potentialities of the staff are further ignored, causing a lessening of motivation throughout the unit. "Heroism sets up a self-defeating cycle: the more the manager accepts the responsibilities for departmental success, the greater the likelihood that subordinates will yield it, forcing the manager to take more, and so on." [p. 17]

In any effort to construct a model of effective leadership, it is important to analyze the heroic manager model. What brought it about? What are its implications? How should we deal with it?

The heroic manager paradigm is rooted in American history and culture. As children, we learned to revere those heroes of the old West who could ride in on their horses and "save the day." Wyatt Earp is a familiar name to most Americans. Even the outlaws, such as the notorious Jesse and Frank James, are viewed by many as heroes of a kind.

Going from horses to helicopters, we find that present-day heroes are replicas of the old West. The success of Rambo-style movies has been witnessed in box office receipts. But the pervasive influence of such movies extends beyond the confines of the theatre. The Rambo doll and associated attire and weaponry start the enculturation process at an early age. And before we realize it, Rambo becomes a cult figure with a large following, young and old alike.

From examples such as these, we come to understand how history and culture have defined our heroes for us, and we come to realize that American culture has tended to extol the virtues of the *individual* who is able to overcome great odds to "save the day." From further study, we come to understand that this idolization of the individual hero is not found in all cultures. We realize that it is a learned phenomenon that characterizes some cultures but not others.

Even though we have just reason for admiring our heroes, we should understand the limitations of heroic managers in organizations. Indeed, Wyatt Earp and Rambo were both regarded as successful in their particular environments, but they may have had difficulty performing as managers at IBM, Sears, or McDonald's.

What happens when replicas of Wyatt Earp and Rambo perchance end up managing a unit within an organization or even the entire organization? Students of leadership behavior report these undesirable outcomes:

1. The heroic manager makes poor use of human resources. In any particular group of employess, we may expect to find no small amount of capability. But because the heroic manager tends to set goals, make decisions, and solve problems on a solo basis, the capabilities of these employees often remain underutilized. Thus, the group as a whole operates on only four cylinders rather than on all eight.

2. The heroic manager fails to develop the potential of the members of the group. With all eyes on the leader, the followers tend to view themselves merely as a supportive cast. Their primary reason for existence in the organization is to support the leader. They are *means* to this end. With the leader playing a solo role in carrying out the leadership functions, the supporting cast carries out its day-to-day role faced with few challenges other than providing the support demanded by the leader. Being cast in the role of "supporters," the staff members will not develop their full potential. What might have been will never come to fruition.

3. The heroic manager fails to develop synergy within the group. Frequently, each member of the group maintains a one-to-one relation with the leader. This is due partly to the leader's behavior but also partly due to the staff's behavior, because each staff member seeks the personal attention of the leader. As a consequence, the opportunity for teamwork is diminished, which usually translates into lessened productivity.

4. The heroic manager fails to develop a backup for his or her position. Such managers convey the impression that they are indispensable and irreplaceable. Consequently, it would be presumptuous on the part of individual staff members to aspire to the leader's position. Can you imagine the folly of Tonto aspiring to someday replace the Lone Ranger? Even though we can point to selected cases where heroic managers have achieved impressive short-term results, we immediately realize the undesirable consequence when the leader departs.

There is no qualified replacement! While upper management
is seeking a qualified replacement, the group flounders.

It seems clear that the weaknesses inherent in the heroic model
outweigh the strengths. But it also seems clear that any model rooted
in several hundred years of history and culture will be highly resis-
tant to change.

What may be the saving grace is that most managers are pragmatists rather than idealists. They are not locked in on one particular
theoretical management model as though it represented absolute
truth. On the contrary, they are seeking approaches that will yield
improved results in the form of increased productivity. If it can be
demonstrated to these managers that there is a superior alternative
to the heroic model, in terms of yielding greater productivity, they
may be convinced.

THE CHANGING ROLE OF THE MANAGER

In his book titled *Team Building*, William Dyer makes special note
of the changing role of the manager:

> The role of the manager has changed significantly in many
> organizations. The strong manager capable of almost
> single-handedly turning around an organization or depart-
> ment, while still a folk hero in the eyes of many, has given
> way to the recent demands of increasingly complex systems
> for managers who are able to pull together people of diverse
> backgrounds, personalities, training, and experience and
> weld them into an effective working group. [p. xi]

The changing role of the manager is from the Lone Ranger paradigm to that of the team builder. Because of increasingly complex
situations, individual managers are no longer able to carry out the
management functions on a solo basis. They must involve others in
the functions of planning, organizing, staffing and staff development,
directing and leading, and evaluating and controlling. It is important to bear in mind that this is not a matter of altruism; it is a matter of necessity.

To illustrate this point of the changing role of the manager, I
would like to tell you about two different managers of my acquaintance. George and Bill were both managers of small software pro-

ducts companies, George in Washington, D.C., and Bill in Columbus, Ohio. Both were marketing three or four primary software products. Both had about 30 employees. Both were very capable individuals. The one significant difference in their situations was that, at the time of my contact, George was managing his company in 1961, and Bill was managing his in 1986. This 25-year time difference resulted in striking differences between their two situations.

One distinct impression that still stands out in my mind is that George, in 1961, was considered an expert in computer technology. I do not mean one particular aspect of computer technology. He was recognized as an expert in the *field* of computer technology. Anyone who had a question about any aspect of digital computers would go to George for the answer.

George's company had a clearly defined organizational structure. The management team consisted of George as president, a marketing manager, a manager of finance, and four managers of the technical groups. This was a common functional structure, which provided clearly defined responsibilities, authority, and accountability. The context for decision making was clear to everyone involved.

The employees within this organizational structure were highly motivated individuals who demonstrated a great deal of company loyalty. They worked as a team to achieve common goals. Voluntary turnover was no more than 10% per year.

George's market was fairly well defined. He had three or four quality products that met the specific needs of particular clients. These clients pointed him to new clients. The company had found its niche in the marketplace.

Back in 1961 I thought that George had a very demanding job. Perhaps he did, but when we compare George's situation to Bill's, we might conclude that George's job was "a piece of cake."

In 1986, Bill found himself caught up in rapidly changing computer technology. Like George, he was marketing three or four primary software products, but in contrast to George, Bill was expending most of his discretionary funds just to keep his products updated. With regard to staying abreast of new computer technology, Bill readily admitted that he was only a generalist, certainly not an expert.

Noteworthy is that Bill's company was involved in only a very small segment of computer technology. Just to stay abreast of new developments in this small segment, four of his senior-level people had divided the segment so as to allow each one to stay abreast of a small portion of the segment. New developments were occurring so rapidly that it was practically impossible for any one person to keep current in more than one narrow area.

Bill's marketing situation was much more complex than George's. Whereas George's market was fairly stable and predictable, Bill's was volatile. Bill often commented, "The competition is climbing out of the woodwork." In addition to the strong domestic competition, the Japanese also were encroaching on his territory. So to compete with the Japanese, he expanded his markets to international territories. To obtain assistance in this endeavor, he established formal agreements with two or three other firms to market his company's products.

Bill's organizational structure was more complex than that of his counterpart's. Whereas George had a simple functional structure, Bill and his managers had decided on a matrix structure. With the products constituting the horizontal dimension and the technical areas the vertical dimension, the matrix provided both stability and flexibility. Nevertheless, the management problems resulting from this structure, especially those concerning authority and accountability, demanded no small amount of Bill's time for resolution.

Bill was faced with a number of human resources problems. First and foremost, he had to concern himself with the high rate of voluntary turnover of his staff, which was running at about 25% in 1986. Even though he provided a reasonable salary-bonus package, his people were constantly recruited by both his competitors and his clients. Further, he had to be ever vigilant to make certain that his managers were complying with EEO requirements. On top of all of this, his computer specialists were "so darned independent." Each one could be described as a free spirit. How could he ever expect to weld this collection of free spirits into a *team* of people working toward common goals?

Then there was a host of miscellaneous management problems: coping with government regulations, dealing with risk assessment, budgeting for liability insurance. It seemed that the list was never ending.

As I present this scenario of the problems facing the modern-day manager, I do not mean to suggest that Bill placed himself in the role of a Victim. He did not. He viewed all of these problems as challenges, on which he seemed to thrive.

Bill's situation is far more complex than George's. Over the same 25-year period, the illustration presented here could be multiplied many times over, regardless of the type of industry. The corollary to this fact is that the problems facing the modern-day manager are too complex for one individual to deal with single-handedly. One person cannot do it alone.

Thus, if tradition-bound managers can be convinced of the superiority of the team model over the heroic model, we may see the light of day. We may witness a transition from the *Lone* Ranger model to the *Team* Ranger model.

TEAM LEADERS

Team leaders are needed in all spheres of organizational life. This includes marketing, R&D, engineering, production, quality assurance, information systems, human resources, accounting and finance, and all the rest. It also includes first-level management, middle-level management, and upper-level management. The need for team leaders is not limited to particular spheres.

We should now address this question: What is meant by "team leadership"? Especially important is the question: How does team leadership differ from heroic leadership?

The concept of team leadership seems to mean different things to different managers. Thus, a useful point of departure is to state what team leadership is *not*.

Team leadership is not pure democratic leadership. Democratic leadership means putting the various decisions up for vote, and the majority rules. Experience shows that if the group leader typically uses this approach for decision making, it will split the group into subgroups, with each subgroup protecting its own turf. Further, I have noted from my own observations of this approach that decisions frequently are put up for a vote before they have been discussed in depth, which means that the group is working at the surface of an issue rather than at the central core. In view of these considerations, we realize that the use of majority rule in decision making is not leadership; it is an abdication of leadership.

Team leadership is not management by committee. The concept of "committee" usually is associated with academic institutions. Committees oftentimes suffer from lack of clear responsibility, authority, and accountability. Consequently, they are hamstrung in their efforts to achieve results. There is little to no relation between management by committee and team leadership.

Team leadership does not mean involving the staff in every management decision. I have known a few inexperienced managers who assumed that team management *ipso facto* meant that the team should be involved in every decision. Because of the large number of management decisions that must be made daily, such an approach would be inefficient and almost impossible to carry out. Team leadership means that the staff members are involved in those *key* decisions that influence their work. This does not necessarily mean that they will *make* the decisions; rather, they will *contribute their ideas* to these decisions. With team leadership, we must bear in mind that the manager in charge is still responsible for the quality of the decisions, as well as for their successful execution.

Team leadership is not manipulative management. Some managers are still possessed by the spirit of Machiavelli. These are managers who want to make their people *think* that they are participating in key decisions when in fact they are not. This type of management is scandalous. Most people would prefer to work for an honest autocrat rather than for a pseudo-participative manager. Team leadership is authentic leadership. "Playing games" with people is not part of the scene.

With regard to what team leadership *is*, it would be difficult to improve upon the definition offered by William Dyer: "Team leadership is the welding of individuals of diverse backgrounds, experience, and personalities into a productive working group." These are the principal elements: (1) taking a diverse group of individuals and (2) building them into a team that (3) is productive. This is perhaps the greatest of all management challenges.

What are the salient characteristics of team leaders? My own exploration of the subject has uncovered these four attributes:

1. **Team leaders place considerable emphasis on team building.** Team leaders realize that they as individuals can accomplish just so much. There is just so much time in a given day. Thus, the key to success is to have a *multiplier effect*. To this end, team leaders spend a great deal of time in building the team. This development is brought about through team goal setting, team decision making, team problem solving, and

organizational development activities. Team leaders evaluate their own performance on the basis of *how well they have developed the team.*

2. **Team leaders understand that the whole is greater than the sum of the parts.** Team leaders appear to be good Gestalt theorists: they realize that "2 plus 2 can equal 5." They first consider the potential contribution of each team member working alone and then identify ways to promote linkages between and among the members to generate a greater total yield. Rather than "catching people doing things wrong," they "catch people working cooperatively," and then they reinforce it.

3. **Team leaders realize that sharing power with their people will increase their own power.** Far too many managers hold a zero-sum view of organizational life. Underlying this view is the assumption that there is a fixed amount of power in any organization. It then follows that, if a manager gives X amount of power to his or her people, then the manager has lost exactly that amount of power. Team leaders readily see through the fallacy of this line of reasoning. They realize that by empowering their people, by giving them *more* power, that they themselves will gain more power. Because the team members are stronger, the leader will be stronger. These team leaders know that the size of the power "pie" is not fixed; it can indeed expand.

4. **Team leaders are not threatened by the sharing of power.** Team leaders tend to be secure persons. They are not threatened easily. As a consequence, they feel confident in surrounding themselves with excellent people, in developing one or more backups for their position, and in sharing their power with their people. They realize that this sharing of power will benefit their people, the organization as a whole, and themselves. This is truly a win-win situation.

A quick review of these four attributes makes it apparent that the team leader is a different type of manager than the heroic leader. A more in-depth review makes it apparent that being an effective team leader calls for higher level skills than those required of the heroic leader. Certainly the heroic leader needs a good understanding of the system which he or she is managing. The team leader needs this understanding, too, but also some additional skills: a working knowledge of two-way communication (with special emphasis on listening), a working knowledge of human behavior, and a working knowledge of group dynamics. In essence, the team leader must be a good *applied psychologist*. This is a tall order, but the fact that many managers have become effective team leaders proves that it can be done.

Now to return to our original question: How does team leadership differ from heroic leadership? What is the *essential* difference? There is a clear-cut answer: Heroic leaders focus on *getting results*, whereas team leaders focus on *building a team* that will get results.

THE PRODUCTIVE TEAM

Effective team leaders appear to have a good grasp of what constitutes a productive team, not only in terms of results achieved but also in terms of the inner workings of such a team. They are able to discern the state of their own team at any point in time: Is is operating as a productive team? Is it operating as a team or as a collection of diverse individuals? Effective team leaders are able to answer these questions, and, if problems exist, they are able to remedy them.

Can we describe the attributes of the productive team? Building on the reports of others as well as my own observations, I have summarized the salient attributes of the productive team. First, it is necessary to define two concepts: "team" and "productive team."

In the book, *Team Building*, William Dyer presents us with a clear definition of a team:

> Teams are collections of people who must rely on group collaboration if each member is to experience the optimum of success and goal achievement. It is obvious that in order to score touchdowns (and prevent the opponent from scoring) a football team has to play together. It should be just as obvious that a work unit or management group must also work together to ensure success. [p. 4]

The key point here is that teams are *collections of people who must rely on group collaboration if each member is to experience the optimum of success and goal achievement*. It is important to bear in mind that there are some situations in which a collection of people reporting to the same manager simply will not meet this requirement. They do not need to collaborate with others in the group to achieve their own goals, and it is futile for the manager to attempt to force collaboration when it is not called for. But these situations are fairly rare. In most instances, the members of a group need to collaborate with each other to achieve their own goals.

Given this view of what is meant by a team, we can now define what is meant by a *productive* team. Here we can employ the same three criteria that were used to define effective leadership. A productive team is one that (1) achieves results; (2) achieves results in an acceptable manner; and (3) achieves results both in the short term and the long term.

With these prefacing remarks, we can now consider the distinctive attributes of the productive team by contrasting the unproductive team and the productive team.

1. Common agreement on high expectations for the team

In the unproductive team we find little agreement on the expectations for the group, or perhaps there is implied agreement, but it is set for mediocrity. In another case the leader may have high expectations for the team, but the team members do not share this commitment.

In the productive team there is common agreement on high expectations for the team. All members have a will to excel. Principal motivators are high standards, quality, and excellence. Mediocrity simply is not tolerated. This is the catchword: "Until something meets our standards of excellence, we won't ship it."

2. A commitment to common goals

Members of the unproductive team have no commitment to common goals. Very likely, the team members have no clear understanding of the group's goals, or the individual team members are working toward different goals.

Members of the productive team have a definite commitment to the achievement of common goals. The goals provide the team members a common focus. All members have a clear understanding of the goals, and they accept the goals. Further, they realize that the goals can be achieved only through a team effort.

3. Assumed responsibility for work that must be done

In the unproductive team each member has a clearly defined

wall around his or her job responsibilities. Any requirement for action that does not fall within this wall is ignored. One frequently hears the age-old response, "Sorry, that's not my job."

In the productive team each member has a defined job but, in addition, has a commitment *to do anything that needs doing.* The walls surrounding the various jobs are pliable, and the greater commitment is to do whatever is necessary to achieve the group goals. All members of the team have internalized the catchword, "If something needs doing, then see to it that it gets done."

4. Honest and open communication

The unproductive team is characterized by sophistry: deception, intrigue, and "playing games." Statements are clearly articulated, but one always wonders what was actually meant by the statements. What was the underlying intent? "What did Joe really mean by that statement?" In this Machiavellian environment of suspicion and intrigue, paranoia reigns.

The productive team is characterized by honest and open communication. Authentic dialogue is the norm. The members openly express their thoughts and feelings, and they feel free to ask questions with the confidence that they will receive honest answers. There are no hidden agendas; everything is aboveboard.

5. Common access to information

In the unproductive team the leader often controls the flow of information. Such a leader realizes that information is power. It then follows that, to gain power over others, one should control the flow of information.

In the productive team there is common access to information. Information is viewed as a vital resource to each member, and it is the leader's responsibility to make certain that every member has the information needed to get the job done. Except for a few highly sensitive matters, the leader's files are open to all team members.

6. A climate of trust

In the unproductive team we often find a lack of trust among the members. The followers do not trust the leader, the leader does not trust the followers, and the followers do not trust each other. This lack of trust is likely to have a crippling effect on the group's performance.

In the productive team there is a climate of trust. Each team member has an instinctive unquestioning belief in the other team members. Trust is the glue that holds the group together, and enlightened managers know that trust begets trust.

7. A general feeling that one can influence what happens

The individual members of the unproductive team feel that they have little or no influence on the course of events. They are mere oarsmen (or oarspersons) on the boat, which is steered by the captain, who is disinclined to solicit ideas from the crew members.

The individual members of the productive team have a definite feeling that they can influence the course of events in their unit. They do not necessarily believe that they can actually *determine* the course of events for the unit as a whole, but they sincerely believe that they can *influence* the course of events. Members of such a team feel confident that they will be listened to by their leader and that their ideas will be taken into consideration.

8. Support for decisions that are made

In the unproductive team there is lack of general support for the decisions once they are made. Often members of such a team reject a given decision simply because they were not consulted on the decision. These team members are then openly critical of the decision during its implementation phase. In extreme cases, they may attempt to sabotage the decision.

In the productive team there is general support for decisions once they are made. On key decisions, the affected parties are given an opportunity to express their thoughts and feelings on the matters at hand. The members have confidence in the sincerity of the leader in soliciting their inputs to the decision. And even though some members may have "come up short" in selling their own ideas, they nevertheless will support the final decision during the period of execution.

9. A win-win approach to conflict management

What is typically found in the unproductive team is either avoidance of conflict or else a win-lose approach to conflict resolution. With avoidance, the conflicts simply are not dealt with, and the problems only worsen. With the win-lose approach, we once again find the zero-sum assumption. The affected parties assume that in every conflict there must be a clear winner and a clear loser. And consistent with Pygmalion, the expectation is converted into reality.

What is typically found in the productive team is a win-win approach to conflict resolution. Both affected parties approach the confrontation with the assumption that each can emerge as a winner. To achieve this desirable state of affairs, the parties use a problem-solving approach in dealing with the conflict. They *jointly explore* alternative ways in which each party might achieve his or her goals, and how each might *help the other* achieve his or her goals.

10. A focus on process as well as results

The unproductive team may or may not focus on results. Typically, however, such a team does not focus on process, that is, on how the team is functioning as a team and what should be done to make it a more productive team. As a consequence, the team does not improve *as a team.*

The productive team focuses on both results and *how* the results are achieved. On a continuing basis, the team members address these questions: (1) How well are we functioning as a team? (2) What barriers are preventing us from being a productive team? and (3) What should we do to become a more productive team? As a consequence, the team continues to improve *as a team.*

In the course of conducting management seminars, I have included these ten attributes in an assessment inventory to allow the seminar participants to evaluate their own teams. (The respondents are either team leaders or team members.) Using a 5-point scale with "5" being high and "1" being low, a perfect score is 50. After administering the inventory to some 2,000 managers over an eight-year period, I have found a total range of scores from a low of 10 to a high of 50. With the majority of scores falling in the 25 to 35 range, most participants readily agree that there is considerable room for improvement in their own teams.

As a result of this activity, I have been especially impressed by two observations. First, those teams that achieve high scores appear to be very productive and also appear *to have fun*. Second, the tremendous impact of a single individual, *the team leader*, on the scores is evident. Perhaps most readers will respond to these two observations by simply thinking, "But of course." Nevertheless, I want to report them because the results are so striking.

I trust that most readers will agree with this conclusion: Given that we can delineate the characteristics of the productive team, it then follows that managers should be able to acquire the skills needed for developing productive teams.

DEVELOPING A PRODUCTIVE TEAM

Building a productive team is no small task. To take an assemblage of diverse personalities and build them into a collaborative team is a challenge of the highest order. Such an effort is certain to encounter obstacles and frustrations along the way. But it also is likely to encounter some pleasurable moments. The important thing is always to keep in mind a vision of the productive team and not be overwhelmed by the obstacles and frustrations.

Building a productive team calls for an incremental approach. Transforming an unproductive team into a productive team can not be achieved through a single bold and imaginative move or through razzle-dazzle. Rather, it is necessary to do many small things over an extended period of time. These are summarized in the 10 guidelines that follow.

1. **Decide on type of team.** In the book, *Game Plans*, Robert Keidel makes interesting comparisons between organizational teams and sports teams. As indicated in Figure 7, he focuses on three different sports teams — baseball, football, and basketball — and shows their counterparts in business and industry. Keidel does not suggest that any particular sports team model is ideal, because any one of them might be appropriate under a given set of circumstances. The point that is emphasized is to know exactly what game your organization or unit is playing — or *should be* playing — and then choose the appropriate model.

2. **Communicate your vision.** We have stressed that one of the chief functions of leadership is to create a clear vision of the desired state of the organization. This vision should be an exciting view of the future that will inspire the members of the team to put forth their best efforts. The important thing is not to keep your vision a secret. Share it with your people and solicit their ideas

on how best to embellish the vision and then convert it into reality. Bear in mind that this is not a one-time activity. The vision must be communicated on a continuing basis through your words, your decisions, and your actions.

3. **Communicate your philosophy of management.** As a manager, you should have a basic philosophy of management: an elucidation of your concept of management and how the management function should be carried out. Included in this philosophy of management should be a clear statement of values, goals, and strategies. It is important that they be consistent and that they

---

BASEBALL: The employees operate independently.

Examples: "Heavy hitting" saleswomen at Mary Kay Cosmetics and basic researchers at Bell Labs.

FOOTBALL: The manager calls all the plays for such organizations.

Examples: McDonald's franchises and automobile assembly plants.

BASKETBALL: The employees coordinate themselves as a flexible group, with the manager as catalyst.

Examples: State-of-the-art computer companies and project teams.

From *Game Plans: Sports Strategies for Business,* by R. Keidel, 1985, p. 6–10. Reprinted with permission of E.P. Dutton, New York, NY.

Figure 7.   What game is your organization playing?

support and reinforce one another. Do not keep your philosophy of management a secret. Share it with your people. They will then understand "where you are coming from." Most important, make certain that your day-to-day decisions and actions are a true echo of your expressed philosophy.

4. **Communicate your positions on key issues.** Bennis and Nanus state it well when they say: "The leader's *positions* must be clear. We tend to trust leaders when we know where they stand in relation to the organization relative to the environment." [p. 154] In most organizations, major issues that affect the organization are being debated day in and day out. Undoubtedly you will form your own opinions on these various issues. Your people will want to know how you stand on these matters. Tell them. And, on a given issue, do not be overly concerned about holding a consistent view over time. As Emerson stated so well: "A foolish consistency is the hobgoblin of little minds."

5. **Involve team members in setting unit objectives.** I believe that most books on management by objectives are missing a vital step in the MBO process. Typically, the author recommends that the beginning point be a meeting between the supervisor and the employee to agree on the employee's performance objectives for the coming review period. What is needed before this meeting is a meeting of the key people in the group in which the team formulates the *unit objectives* for the coming year. This would then be followed by the one-on-one meetings between the supervisor and each employee to agree on the employee's performance objectives, which should be written *to support the unit objectives.*

6. **Involve team members in developing strategies.** Once the unit objectives are formulated for the coming year, it is then necessary to formulate strategies on how best to achieve the objectives. It might be tempting for you as a manager to sit in your office and develop these strategies single-handedly. Resist the temptation! Set up a meeting in which you and your people formulate the strategies on a team basis. Assuming that your people have relevant knowledge and experience, the chances are good that you will generate better strategies than what you would have accomplished alone. Most important is that your people will all say, "We did this ourselves."

7. **Involve team members in solving problems.** There should be many opportunities for involving your people in problem-solving activities on a team basis. This does not mean that you should involve your people every time a problem arises. It does mean, however, that you should involve them when they are likely to make a significant contribution and when it is important to get their ownership of the solution. A suggested strategy for a team problem-solving meeting is shown in Figure 8, which is an adaptation of one developed by Human Synergistics. The ability to

---

1. Clearly state the problem.

2. Describe the situation (including any relevant history) as it now exists.

3. Describe what you hope the situation will be like if the problem solving effort has a successful outcome.

4. Describe what the situation will be like if the problem solving effort is unsuccessful.

5. List the benefits that will result from a successful outcome.

6. List the resources that will be required to achieve that outcome.

7. List the driving forces that may help solve the problem.

8. List the restraining forces that may prevent the problem from getting solved.

9. Develop strategies for solving the problem.

10. Develop an action plan that should produce the desired outcome.

From *Leader's Manual: Solving Problems and Planning for Change,* 1985. Reprinted with permission of Human Synergistics, Plymouth, Michigan.

Figure 8.   A strategy for solving problems.

take the team through the entire process, until the team develops its own action plan for solving the problem, is a high-level leadership skill.

8. **Involve team members in key decisions.** Certainly there will be many opportunities for involving your people in key decisions. Again, it would be inappropriate to involve them in every decision. But you should involve them whenever the decision is likely to have a significant impact on their jobs. In a decision-making meeting with your people, you might consider any one of these approaches: (1) present to them a problem, solicit their ideas, and you make the decision; (2) present to them a tentative decision that is subject to change based upon their inputs; (3) present to them several alternatives and let them choose what they consider to be the best alternative; or (4) present to them a problem situation and let them generate the alternatives and even choose the preferred alternative. Depending on the circumstances, any one of these approaches might be appropriate. The important thing is to let your people know *up front* which approach you are using.

9. **Involve team members in reviewing progress and deciding upon corrective action.** With the heroic leadership approach, the leader is diligent in monitoring group performance and deciding upon corrective action. In most situations, a more effective approach would be to involve the team members in this activity. This latter approach will be superior to the heroic approach for a least two reasons: (1) the ideas of the people on the "firing line" are likely to improve the quality of the decisions regarding corrective action; and (2) the motivation of the people on the firing line to implement the decisions will surely be enhanced.

10. **Involve team members in a team-building program.** You should set aside at least one day each year for a team-building program. Involve your key people in the all-day meeting and, if possible, get away from the work site. The primary purpose of this meeting is to formulate recommendations for being a more productive team. To be addressed are these questions: (1) How well are we functioning as a team? (2) What barriers are preventing us from being a productive team? and (3) What actions should we take to become a more productive team? A suggested agenda for such a meeting is shown in Figure 9. Whether or not you have ever

1. Get away from the work site for one day.

2. Each person writes answers to these questions:

   (a) What keeps you from being as effective as you would like to be in your position?

   (b) What keeps the staff (unit or department) from functioning as an effective team?

   (c) What do you like about this unit that you want to maintain?

   (d) What suggestions do you have for improving the quality of our working relationships and the functioning of our department?

3. Responses are recorded on flipcharts.

4. Group sets priorities on problems they want to address.

5. Group begins working on high-priority problems.

6. A time is set for follow-up.

From *Strategies for Managing Change*, by W. Dyer, 1984, p. 124–125. Reprinted with permission of Addison-Wesley Publishing Co., Reading, MA.

Figure 9. A team building program.

been involved in such a meeting, I believe that you will find that conducting an annual team-building program with your people will pay great dividends.

These 10 guidelines can be applied by any manager who desires to be an effective team leader. If the guidelines are applied in a conscientious and consistent manner, the beneficial results should become readily apparent.

BENEFITS OF A TEAM APPROACH

Let's suppose that you want to make a genuine commitment to being an effective team leader. What are the implications of such a commitment? Certainly, if done conscientiously, you can expect some beneficial results. Even if the commitment is carried out in a conscientious manner, however, you also may encounter some drawbacks such as excessive time requirements for the active involvement of your staff, the possible compromising of decisions, and the possible creation of open conflict. Without minimizing the significance of these drawbacks, it seems evident that the expected benefits of team leadership far outweigh the potential drawbacks.

The expected benefits of a team approach to leadership are shown in the conceptual framework of Figure 10. Within this cause-and-

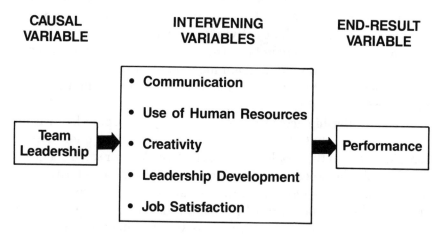

Figure 10.   Benefits of team leadership.

effect model, we can expect effective team leadership to have a positive impact on at least five intervening variables: (1) communication, (2) use of human resources, (3) creativity, (4) leadership development, and (5) job satisfaction. Enhancement of these five intervening variables should then have a positive impact on performance. Thus, team leadership has a positive impact on performance *via* these intervening variables.

In contrasting team leadership and heroic leadership, we can expect team leadership to yield the following positive results.

Team leadership brings about improved communication. Heroic leadership focuses on one-way communication, (i.e., top-down), whereas team leadership focuses on two-way communication. Involvement of the staff in goal setting, problem solving, decision making, and progress review definitely enhances the communication process. By being actively involved in these activities, the team members are kept informed all along the way, and the leader benefits by hearing the concerns of the staff and getting their inputs all along the way. This ongoing two-way exchange is far superior to the heroic leader's monthly staff meetings in which the leader conveys the happenings of the past month (with special placed emphasis on his or her accomplishments).

Team leadership makes better use of human resources. In practically any group of people in organizational settings, there is a considerable amount of talent, either manifest or latent, that can contribute to the task at hand. Why not capitalize on this talent in such activities as goal setting, problem solving, decision making, and progress review? Each of these activities can benefit from the active involvement of the team members, from the *unique and valuable* contribution of each individual team member. Here the leader will be able to demonstrate that the whole is indeed greater than the sum of its parts.

Team leadership generates more creativity. Most of us know from past experience that often "two heads are better than one." This is especially true in the development of creative ideas for solving a given problem. As the process unfolds, one person presents a tentative idea; another person piggybacks on the initial idea and suggests a more substantial idea; then a third person builds on the second person's idea; and so the process continues. As we examine the outcome of this process, it is apparent that no one person in the group could have generated this particular solution to the problem single-handedly. It was clearly the result of a team effort.

Team leadership brings about better leadership development. One of the most effective ways for a young manager to learn how to be an effective leader is to observe an effective leader in action, to have a role model. In the case of heroic leadership, the young manager has little opportunity to witness first-hand how the problem solving process is worked through or how the decisions are actually arrived at. But with team leadership, the young manager is able to witness first-hand how these leadership processes unfold. This is learning at its best.

Team leadership leads to improved job satisfaction. We know from a great deal of empirical research and first-hand observations that there are identifiable factors associated with team leadership that contribute to job satisfaction: knowing what is going on, feeling that you are being listened to, being able to influence decisions, and feeling that you are a vital member of the team, to name a few. The presence or absence of these factors can spell the difference between being enthusiastic about going to work in the morning versus preferring to pull the sheet over your head and going back to sleep.

Collectively, these five intervening variables can be expected to have a substantial impact on performance. If a team scores high on communication, use of human resources, creativity, leadership development, and job satisfaction, then surely we can expect to find a correspondence in performance, in both individual performance and group performance. Conversely, if a team scores low on these five intervening variables, then we can again expect to find a correspondence in performance. And who is the single most important individual who has the power to influence the scores? Obviously, the leader.

In summing up, I ask you to reflect on your own leadership style. To what extent *are you* a team leader? To what extent *should you be* a team leader? To what extent would you *like to be* a team leader? If you decide to make a commitment to being a more effective team leader, *then do it.* Lay out a plan for yourself and then convert the plan into reality through your day-to-day decisions and actions.

As you consider your role as a leader, reflect on these words of wisdom offered by an early writer on leadership, Mary Parker Follett:

The leader is one who can organize the experience of the

group — whether it be the small group of the foreman, the larger group of the department, or the whole plant — can organize the experience of the group and thus get the full power of the group. The leader makes the team. This is preeminently the leadership quality — the ability to organize all the forces there are in an enterprise and make them serve a common purpose. (*Freedom and Coordination*, p. 52)

V

Clarifying the Values

Every man should expend his chief thought and attention
on his first principles: Are they or are they not rightly laid
down? And when he has duly sifted them, all the rest will
follow rightly.

Socrates
Cratylus

---

*Importance of Corporate Values • When Values Are Not in Harmony • An
Illustration of Corporate Values • Identifying the Critical Success Factors
• Translating Values into Practice • How Shared Values Affect Performance*

IMPORTANCE OF CORPORATE VALUES

The importance of corporate values is underscored by Thomas Watson, Jr. in this IBM credo:

> I firmly believe that any organization, in order to survive
> and achieve success, must have a sound set of beliefs on
> which it premises all its policies and actions.
>
> Next, I believe that the most important factor in corporate success is faithful adherence to those beliefs.
>
> And finally, I believe that if an organization is to meet
> the challenges of a changing world, it must be prepared
> to change everything about itself except those beliefs as it
> moves through corporate life. (in Pascale and Athos, *The
> Art of Japanese Management,* p. 184)

Every organization is guided by certain beliefs or values. These values communicate to all members "what we stand for" and "what is important to us." Whether the values are explicit or implicit, they constitute the essence of the organization's management philosophy. Values are the soul of the organization.

One sign of a healthy organizational culture is congruence between the organization's statement of values and the daily behavior of its members. Conversely, one sign of an organizational culture in trouble is lack of congruence between the organization's statement of values and the daily behavior of its members. It is clear that every enterprise needs an explicit statement of organizational values and the witnessing of these values in the day-to-day actions of its members.

In the popular book, *In Search of Excellence*, Thomas Peters and Robert Waterman highlight the importance of translating organizational values into practice:

> Let us suppose that we were asked for one all-purpose bit of advice for management, one truth that we were able to distill from the excellent companies research. We might be tempted to reply, "Figure out your value system. Decide what your company *stands for*." Clarifying the value system and breathing life into it are the greatest contributions a leader can make. [p. 279, p. 291]

A useful conceptual framework for relating organizational values and practice is shown in Figure 11. Stanley Davis provides a cause-

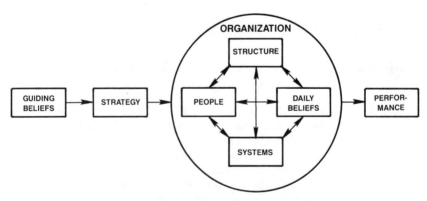

From *Managing Corporate Culture*, by S. Davis, 1984, p. 6, The Human Resource Planning Company. Reprinted with permission of Ballinger Publishing Company, Cambridge, MA.

Figure 11. Two dimensions of culture: guiding beliefs and daily beliefs.

and-effect model consisting of three classes of variables: antecedent, intervening, and outcome. The antecedent variables include the guiding beliefs (i.e., organizational values) and the strategy. Included as intervening variables are the structure, the people, the systems, and the daily beliefs. The outcome variables include various performance measures, indicators of success for the organization as a whole.

The focal point of Davis's model is the relation between the guiding beliefs and the daily beliefs:

> *Guiding beliefs* are the roots and principles upon which the company is built, the philosophical foundation of the corporation. As fundamental precepts, guiding beliefs rarely change. They are held in the realm of universal truths, and are broad enough to accommodate any variety of circumstances.
>
> *Daily Beliefs*, on the other hand, are a different species. While they are equally part of a corporation's culture, they should not be confused with guiding beliefs. Daily beliefs are rules and feelings about everyday behavior. They are situational and change to meet circumstances. They tell people the ropes to skip and the ropes to know. They are the survival kit for the individual. [p. 4]

The underlying premise of the model is that the degree of congruence between guiding beliefs and daily beliefs will have a significant impact on overall organizational performance. A high degree of relation between guiding beliefs and daily beliefs will contribute positively to organizational performance. Conversely, a low degree of relation between these two sets of beliefs will contribute negatively to organizational performance.

Thus, for each manager there is a clear challenge: Do whatever is reasonably possible to assure a high degree of congruence between the organization's guiding beliefs and the members' daily beliefs. First, the guiding beliefs must be clearly communicated to all members of the organization. Next, these guiding beliefs must be put into practice on a daily basis. In the ideal case, the guiding beliefs and the daily beliefs, while perhaps not identical, are in harmony.

WHEN VALUES ARE NOT IN HARMONY

Suppose that you are listening to an orchestra that is not in harmony.

After listening to the discordance for a few moments, you become aware that something is terribly amiss. It appears that the musicians are not following the same musical score. It even appears that some of the members are not following any score at all. What is most disconcerting is that the leader sometimes follows the score and sometimes does not. Even the score itself seems to be incongruous — a crazy mixture of classical, jazz, and hard rock. How long would you remain at this bizarre event? Probably not very long. Only a masochist would remain.

If we equate "musical score" and "organizational values," this situation is not unlike that which is found in some organizations. Just as the score is important to the performance of the members of the orchestra, the values are important to members of the organization. As indicated in Figure 12, we can be assured that harmony in values will have a positive impact on performance, whereas discord in values will have a negative impact. What is meant by "harmony in values"? We mean essentially two things: the values of the organization are all of a piece, and the values of the organization and the behavior of its members are consistent.

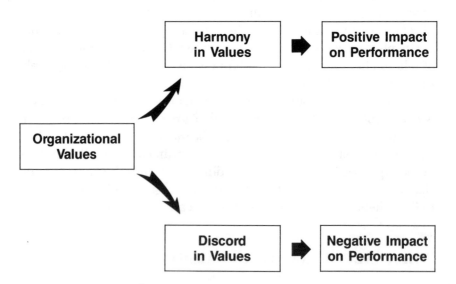

Figure 12. Relation between values and performance.

We do not have to look far to find examples of discordance in organizational values. Readily apparent are these examples:

1. Incongruity between the statement of organizational values and the real understanding of these values on the part of the members.

2. Incongruity between the values of one unit and those of another unit within the same organization.

3. Incongruity between the statement of organizational values and the behavior of the organization's leaders.

The existence of any one of these incongruities would be reason for concern. An organization plagued with all three simultaneously would be considered a sick organization. In the language of Terence Deal and Allan Kennedy, it would be "a culture in trouble."

Incongruity between the statement of organizational values and the real understanding of these values on the part of the members should be reason for concern. Consider the situation in which upper management issues a statement of corporate values to all staff members and assumes that its job of communicating the values has been accomplished. This seems like a simple matter, doesn't it? Not really. What was meant by the particular values in the minds of upper management may not be the same as what is assumed in the minds of the staff. With regard to "quality," for example, upper management means that every project should "satisfy the performance requirements." If the performance requirements called for a good Chevrolet, then this is what is to be produced. But then some of the technical staff interpret "quality" to mean "exceeds performance requirements" and only a Cadillac could do this; a Chevrolet would be unacceptable. Further, upper management intended that quality be defined in terms of three criteria: technical performance, schedule, and budget. The technical staff, however, may assume that quality refers only to technical performance, and that it may be acceptable to overrun in schedule or budget. And so it goes. As most managers know, communication is the key.

Incongruity between the values of one unit and those of another within the same organization should be reason for concern. In some organizations, it appears that each unit is listening to the beat of a different drummer. This would not necessarily be bad if the various units could function effectively as independent entities; but if the various units must function as a collective entity, as a team, then the discordance will create severe problems. Assume, for example, that there are three different organizational units participating in the same project. Assume further that one unit places primary emphasis on technical performance, the second on schedule, and the third on budget. We have just gone from classical to jazz to hard rock. Under these conditions, the project manager, who may have little formal authority across the three units, can be expected to age rapidly.

Incongruity between the statement of organizational values and the behavior of the organization's leaders should be reason for concern. Of the three different types of incongruities, this one may be the most damaging. Consider the company that includes in its written statement of values that "people are our most important resource" but behaves in such a manner to suggest that it is not truly committed to this value. The decisions and actions of upper management would strongly indicate that quarterly profits are the only real concern. When it comes to setting actual priorities, it is obvious that employees and their welfare are nowhere near the top of the totem pole. This blatant insincerity takes its toll on staff morale and voluntary turnover, and eventually, on productivity. Small wonder that in some companies, the major human relations problem is *lack of trust of upper management.*

Our question now becomes: What is the overall impact of these incongruities? What happens if the orchestra members do not understand the musical score? Or if the members are following different scores? Or if the leader ignores the score? Well, to say the least, we have a bad situation, a very bad situation.

At a minimum, we can expect to find these consequences: inconsistency and fragmentation, lack of overall direction, lack of a sense of stability, lack of a consistent framework for decision making, lack of trust, lack of social cohesion and esprit de corps, low employee motivation and morale, all of which contribute to lowered productivity. These are indeed grave consequences, which are sufficiently weighty to warrant serious consideration on the part of every manager.

Is there a way out? I think so, *assuming the proper commitment from management.* It is up to upper management and all managers down the line to do everything reasonably possible to assure harmony of values. We should be reminded of the message from Thomas Peters and Robert Waterman: "Clarifying the value system and breathing life into it are the greatest contributions a leader can make."

AN ILLUSTRATION OF CORPORATE VALUES

In the course of conducting management seminars, I often have been asked this question: "What does a statement of corporate values look like?" Assuming that you, the reader, may have the same question, I will use Battelle's values as an illustration of corporate values. I make this choice for three reasons: (1) Battelle has a lucid statement of values; (2) the statement of values could serve as a model for other organizations; and (3) I am very familiar with these values.

Battelle is a large nonprofit organization that provides contracted services in research, development, and program management on an international basis. The organization was established in 1929 on the basis of a will written by its founder, Gordon Battelle.

Battelle grew and prospered over a 50-year period without any written statement of corporate values. Yet it seemed apparent that there was indeed a set of values implicit in the organization's culture. Then, in 1982, the executive vice president of the organization, Dr. Ronald Paul, took it upon himself to make the values explicit. By reviewing many written documents, including the Gordon Battelle Will, past writings of Battelle's leaders, and several strategic plans, Dr. Paul was able to formulate a first draft of Battelle values. He then sought comments on this first draft from a large number of Battelle staff.

The end result of this effort was a clear statement of eight Battelle values. Embedded in the Battelle logo, these eight values are shown in Figure 13. The values are elucidated in Dr. Paul's paper, "Battelle Values," which was published in March, 1982, as a *BMI Bulletin*. Presented below are large portions of the paper.

BENEFIT TO HUMANITY—Battelle's operations always must be oriented toward solving the problems and serving the needs of others.

> Battelle exists to serve mankind through the capabilities of science and technology. Generally we serve particular segments of society through intermediaries—our clients. In proposing, performing, and delivering sponsored work, we must strive to understand the needs of the clients— from their viewpoints. Their needs, not ours, should determine if and how we do the work, and how and when we deliver the results.

INNOVATION — Battelle aspires to institutional leadership in scientific discovery, technical inventiveness, and technological innovation.

> Collectively, Battelle staff members must not only have a sound knowledge of scientific, engineering, and professional principles, but also must be contributors to the advancement of such knowledge through creative theoretical and experimental studies, analysis, and interpretation. Our attitude toward problems must not be one of despair, but rather one of challenge that "there must be a better way," and one of confidence that we have the competence and creativity to find it and prove it.

INTEGRITY — We expect ethical behavior on the part of all staff members.

> One way or another, all the activities of Battelle are built upon the accumulating knowledge of science. Good science

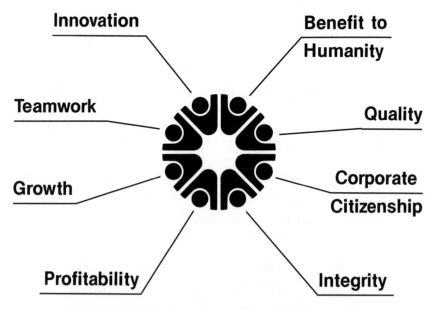

Figure 13.   Battelle values. The Battelle logo symbolizes an interdisciplinary team of scientists and engineers working on a common problem and then communicating the results to the outside world.

is absolutely dependent upon objective, honest observation, analysis, and reporting. Thus, lack of integrity
or less than ethical behavior in any aspect of our
business performance casts a shadow on the credibility
of the technical work through which we earn our right
to institutional existence. Decisions and actions must
consistently be beyond question from an ethical
standpoint.

QUALITY—The hallmark of Battelle's activities must be services and
products of the highest quality commensurate with the needs and
resources of those who pay for them.

> All staff members are responsible for continually improv-
> ing their skills so their individual work will always meet
> or exceed the standards of their vocation or profession.
> Managers are responsible for organizing, integrating, and
> leading these individual efforts to assure that Battelle always
> provides services and products which meet the highest
> quality standards feasible within the time and money con-
> straints of the task. We should be known as results-oriented
> problem solvers.

TEAMWORK—A distinctive and desired characteristic of Battelle
is the ability to transform acts of creativity and inventiveness by individuals into high-quality services and products of value through
the teamwork of diversely talented staff members dedicated to
achievement of a common objective.

> Because Battelle is large and complex, a formal and more
> or less permanent organizational structure is needed for the
> orderly conduct of our business. Nevertheless, Battelle has
> great strength in its capability for transcending organiza-
> tional boundaries and quickly forming cohesive working
> teams of persons who respect and trust each other, and have
> enthusiasm for working together to meet a shared challenge.

CORPORATE CITIZENSHIP—Battelle aspires to honor its obliga-
tions to society by being an economic, intellectual, and social asset
to each nation and each community in which it operates.

> Managers are accountable for conceiving, planning, and
> leading the visible manifestations of our corporate citizen-
> ship. We must serve not only the communities in which we

live, but also the broader technical, national, and international communities in which we work. Of no less importance are the less visible, wholly voluntary, donated services of many staff members to a wide variety of worthy professional, civic, charitable, and religious enterprises.

GROWTH — A world of increasing population, complexity, and interdependence needs a Battelle that also is growing and advancing in capabilities for serving societal needs.

> We interpret our founder's charge to assure the advancement of the Institute to include growth in size as well as growth in quality and service. Institutional growth is required for serving societal needs, and also for providing a quality work environment for our staff. Such an environment will offer increasing opportunities for staff members who seek more responsibility as individual contributors or managers, a richness of opportunities for work assignments diverse in content and location, and a work community that is dynamic rather than lethargic.

PROFITABILITY — For Battelle to continue and advance, it is necessary, but not sufficient, that we generate the retained earnings needed to achieve our objectives, and thus serve our public purposes.

> Without continuing fiscal viability, Battelle would eventually cease to exist. Retained earnings, or profit, are earned by supplying our clients with something of real worth. Our objective must be to provide services and products which merit payments that include profit, not just recovery of costs. Our clients understand and accept that objective, as it is necessary for all viable businesses.

* * * *

> From discussions with many staff members and through introspection, it is apparent that when there is substantial compatibility between one's personal values and the desired Battelle values, and all are in reasonable balance, then there also is excitement, enjoyment, and a fuller sense of self-realization in one's work.

IDENTIFYING THE CRITICAL SUCCESS FACTORS

In translating values into practice, we must move from the abstract to the concrete, from the general to the specific. Managers want to know what they can *actually do* to satisfy the values. They want to know what specific actions they can take to make certain that the values are fulfilled.

While it is clear that such values as benefit to humanity, innovation, quality, corporate citizenship, etc., may have considerable motivational appeal, they must be defined in more specific terms to allow managers to understand them. They must be defined in sufficiently specific terms to suggest specific actions on the part of the managers.

A useful method for helping us move from the abstract to the concrete is found in the identification of "critical success factors." The critical success factor method was developed by information specialists as a means of identifying the specific information needs of managers. The method seems readily adaptable to our present task.

In the booklet, *A Primer on Critical Success Factors*, Christine Bullen and John Rockart offer this definition of critical success factors:

> Critical success factors are the limited number of areas in which satisfactory results will ensure successful competitive performance for the individual, department, or organization. CSFs are the few key areas where "things must go right" for the business to flourish and for the manager's goals to be attained. [p. 7]

These two authors stress that, in every manager's job, there are an extremely large number of factors to which his or her attention can be directed. The key to success for managers is to focus their most limited resource, their time, on those factors that really spell the difference between success and failure.

It is generally accepted that most managers have implicit critical success factors that they have been using, "most often subconsciously," to help them manage throughout their careers. Through in-depth interviews of managers, it is possible to make these critical success factors *explicit*. Once the critical success factors are made explicit, it is possible to establish clear priorities and focus attention on specific contributory actions.

Bullen and Rockart suggest some practical questions that may be asked of the manager to elicit his or her critical success factors:

1. "Will you tell me, in whatever order they come to mind, those things that you see as critical success factors in your job at this time?"

2. "Let me ask the same question concerning critical success factors in another way. In what one, two, or three areas would failure to perform well hurt you the most? In short, where would you most hate to see something go wrong?"
3. "Assume you are placed today in a dark room with no access to the outside world, except for food and water. What would you most want to know about the business when you came out three months later?"

Using this method, I asked Battelle managers to identify the critical success factors associated with each of the eight Battelle values. Managers were presented with this question: What specific actions on the part of Battelle managers will determine whether or not each value is satisfied? Conducting this exercise with 80 Battelle managers representing all five Battelle components produced an excellent list of critical success factors. The review and editing of this material resulted in the CSFs shown in Figure 14.

These critical success factors represent the specific areas that should receive attention by managers to assure the fulfillment of each value. It should be noted that these CSFs are not definitive, but merely suggestive. A more definitive listing might present different CSFs for different levels of management. Also, the CSFs would be expected to vary somewhat from division to division and between research departments and support departments. The intent here, however, is to focus less on content and more on process.

The key idea is that the critical success factor method is a practical approach for helping us move from the abstract to the concrete — to identify those specific areas that will ensure successful performance in the light of the values.

TRANSLATING VALUES INTO PRACTICE

What should be done to make certain that organizational values are put into practice? More specifically, what should each manager do to assure that the values are translated into a reality that is manifest in the staff's daily behavior?

It is generally agreed that the manager serves as the focal point for the organization's value system. Staff members look to the manager for cues to determine what constitutes acceptable and unac-

BENEFIT TO HUMANITY	INNOVATION

BENEFIT TO HUMANITY

- Identify important societal problems.
- Properly define important societal problems.
- Market programs that will help solve significant societal problems.
- Manage resources to solve significant societal problems.
- Evaluate performance on basis of solving significant societal problems.

INNOVATION

- Have a visionary, future-directed outlook.
- Hire innovative staff members.
- Establish an environment that fosters innovation.
- Be willing to risk.
- Be willing to invest.

QUALITY

- Recruit high-quality staff.
- Acquire and maintain up-to-date equipment.
- Establish a formal Quality Assurance (QA) system.
- Carefully review all proposals and reports.
- Involve client in the project.

TEAMWORK

- Set example by day-to-day actions and conversations.
- Develop knowledge of capabilities and needs of other groups.
- Acknowledge the strengths and weaknesses of your group.
- Promote win-win solutions rather than win-lose solutions.
- Reward teamwork - don't punish.

CORPORATE CITIZENSHIP

- Encourage staff to publish in professional journals.
- Encourage staff to participate in professional societies.
- Encourage staff to participate in activities of the local community.
- Serve as a role model for staff by participating in activities of the local community.
- Help obtain the resources needed by staff to participate in professional and community activities.

GROWTH

- Establish a long-range plan to guide the group's activities.
- Focus resources on selected technical areas.
- Align organizational structure to changing environment.
- Actively promote and support staff development activities.
- Be willing to "fold" in a given technical area and redirect resources.

INTEGRITY

- Set an example by consistently acting with integrity.
- Hire people with personal integrity.
- Demand integrity as a performance requirement.
- Make certain that all proposals and reports reflect a high degree of integrity.
- Take action promptly in dealing with staff who demonstrate lack of integrity.

PROFITABILITY

- Communicate to staff the idea that profit in a not-for-profit organization is essential for survival and growth.
- Price projects realistically so that they generate a net profit.
- Endeavor to achieve the optimal time on projects for all staff.
- Make effective and efficient use of overhead funds.
- Assure that projects meet clients' needs and are completed within budget and schedule.

Figure 14.   Critical success factors associated with Battelle values.

ceptable behavior within the organization. The daily decisions and actions of the manager reflect more than anything else the organization's *actual values*. Therefore, it is incumbent on you as a manager to understand fully the organization's values, to internalize these values, and to live the values on a daily basis.

The principal mode of translating values into practice is through effective leadership. In the language of James MacGregor Burns, the challenge for each manager is to be a transforming leader. This is accomplished by raising people from their lower selves to their higher selves. Help your people move up Maslow's hierarchy from survival to safety to belongingness to self-esteem to self-actualization.

As a strategy for translating the values into practice, you should focus on three interrelated avenues: balancing, communicating, and rewarding. We will look at each.

You can help your people move up Maslow's hierarchy by maintaining a *balanced view* of all of the organizational values. The total set must be kept in proper perspective. When times are tough and it may be necessary to give special attention to one particular value (such as profitability), *do not lose sight of the others*. This demand for a balanced view requires that you be ever vigilant.

Here we can appreciate the distinction between the transactional leader and the transforming leader. The transactional leader is likely to focus on those values that are measurable because they allow for a clear exchange of one thing for another. But the transforming leader will take these values as "givens" while at the same time attending to the more qualitative values. The transforming leader realizes the importance of all of the organizational values for the long-term success of the organization. These values are viewed as *a set of interrelated elements*, which means that the various values are mutually supportive and that no one of the values can be sacrificed without disrupting the total set.

As an integral part of the leadership function, you should communicate on an ongoing basis the importance of the organizational values every day and every opportunity. This communication may take a variety of forms: interpersonal communication, group meetings, written communication, and even body language. And it is a truism that the manager is actually communicating even when he or she decides *not* to communicate. Communication takes place through both words and actions, and most would agree that actions or the absence thereof speak louder than words.

Whenever you are inquiring about performance — or simply, "How are things going?" — you should be especially attentive to the nature and scope of the questions. For instance, if the questions are limited to profitability, this restrictive interest will signal to your staff your principal, and perhaps only, priority. On the other hand, if your questions are broadened to cover additional organizational values, this expansive interest will signal a very different set of priorities.

Similarly, whenever you present a report to your people on the group's performance, special attention should be given to the scope of the topics covered. If the progress report focuses only on bottom-line financial performance, the staff will clearly understand your sole priority. On the other hand, if such a presentation is expanded to cover progress on critical success factors associated with other organizational values, the staff will receive a completely different message. Communication is the key.

Considering a specific example of communication, all managers should bear in mind that the organization's reward system clearly communicates to the staff the relative importance of the organization's different values. And we know that the reward system includes more than pay and promotions. It also includes opportunity to receive further training, freedom to pursue a special interest, being given greater responsibility and authority, or simply hearing the supervisor remark, "That's great!"

You should give special attention to the particular type of performance that is being rewarded. Are staff members rewarded only for being profitable? Or are they also rewarded for turning out quality products or services, for being innovative, for being good team players, for demonstrating high integrity, and for being good community citizens? We know from experience that the reward system is a powerful vehicle for communicating the organization's value system. The challenge for each manager is to use it effectively.

HOW SHARED VALUES AFFECT PERFORMANCE

In their book *Corporate Cultures*, Deal and Kennedy stress that successful companies place a great deal of emphasis on values. They found that these companies share three characteristics:

- They stand for something — that is, they have a clear and ex-

plicit philosophy about how they aim to conduct their business.
- Management pays a great deal of attention to shaping and fine-tuning these values to conform to the economic and business environment of the company and to communicating them to the organization.
- These values are known and shared by all the people who work for the company — from the production worker right through the ranks of senior management. [p. 22]

It seems clear that the test of a healthy organizational culture is harmony in values. "Harmony in values" means two things: The values of the organization are internally consistent, and the values of the organization and the behavior of its members are consistent.

As indicated in Figure 15, achieving harmony in values involves five key elements: the organizational values, the critical success factors, balancing, communicating, and rewarding. The proposed management strategy for linking these five elements includes the following measures:

1. Develop a written statement of organizational values.
2. Identify the critical success factors associated with each value.
3. Maintain a balanced view of all of the organizational values.
4. Communicate the values on an ongoing basis through words and actions.
5. Establish a reward system that reinforces those behaviors that support the values.

Implementing this broad-based strategy is no simple task. But it can be done. In fact, in some quarters it *is* being done. And if something *is* being done, then it *can* be done.

Assuming success in this endeavor, one can expect these desirable outcomes:

1. Harmony in values will provide a sense of common direction for all staff and guidelines for their daily behavior. Peter Drucker has likened the job of the manager to that of the orchestra leader. This is an apt metaphor. Perhaps an equally apt metaphor is that between the *organizational values* and the *musical score*. Even though the staff may be versatile, they still need to know what kind of music they are to play — classical, jazz, or hard rock. Without a clear and consistent

signal on this matter, there will be a great deal of noise but little music.

2. Harmony in values will provide the social energy and esprit de corps that moves the organization into action. Perhaps the organization will be able to move from state A to state B merely by means of physical energy. But certainly it will move more rapidly and more successfully if the physical energy is supplemented by social energy. Social energy is generated whenever a group of people are working together *as a community of persons with a common center.* This common center denotes the organizational values, and the radii represent the commitment of the individual members to these organizational values. Here we find esprit de corps at its best.

3. Harmony in values will permit upper management to influence employee behavior without being present physically.

Figure 15.   Key elements in achieving harmony in values.

It would be almost impossible for upper management always to be physically present to oversee the work of the employees. And even if it were possible, it would be highly undesirable from a motivational standpoint. But there is a definite way for upper management to have a profound impact on the behavior of every member of the organization at all times: by clearly communicating the values and doing everything reasonably possible to win a commitment to these values through the internalization of the values on the part of every staff member. If upper management is successful in this endeavor, then the organizational values will serve as the *collective conscience* for all members of the organization.

4. Harmony in values will provide a framework for managerial decision making. In the making of managerial decisions, the organizational values serve as a *gyroscope*, an apparatus capable of maintaining the same absolute direction in space in spite of the movements of the mountings and surrounding parts. Managers make decisions day in and day out, perhaps almost every hour of each day. Effective managers make decisions in accord with a structured rationale, a rationale that includes broad goals, priorities, and weighted criteria. If these managers had to create this rationale for each particular decision, they would be functioning as psychological cripples. What saves them from this malady is that their decision making is guided by the organizational values.

5. Harmony in values will provide a sense of stability and continuity in a rapidly changing environment. Practically all human beings have a basic need for stability and continuity. Because large numbers of organizations are now undergoing periods of rapid change, we become even more aware of this basic human need. And it is apparent from all projections that these changes will accelerate even more in the future. Many managers are sensitive to the need to help their employees maintain a reasonable level of sanity in the ever-changing world. The key is to communicate the organizational values as *enduring ideals*. Even though the vessel is moving hither and yon across a tumultuous sea, the values will provide the gyroscope.

Achieving these five desirable outcomes through harmony in

values will be no mean achievement. Indeed, they can easily spell the difference between failure and success, and between despair and joy.

Here we can do no better than end with a relevant quotation from Deal and Kennedy:

> The future holds promise for strong culture companies. Strong cultures are not only able to respond to an environment, but they also adapt to diverse and changing circumstances. When times are tough, these companies can reach deeply into their shared values and beliefs for the truth and courage to see them through. When new challenges arise, they can adjust. This is exactly what companies are going to have to do as we begin to experience a revolution in the structure of modern organizations. [pp. 195–96]

VI

Positioning

A person who does not think and plan long ahead will find
trouble right by his door.

Confucius
The Analects

---

*The Most Demanding Part of Planning • The Problem of Action Without
Strategy • The Essence of Strategy • Attributes of Effective Strategy • On
Developing Strategy • Benefits of a Clear Strategy*

THE MOST DEMANDING PART OF PLANNING

The management function of planning is the foundation and framework for all of the other management functions. Clearly important
are the functions of organizing, staffing and staff development, directing and leading, and evaluating and controlling. Without the function of planning to guide them, however, these functions are certain
to be carried out in an aimless manner.

Managers vary considerably in their perceptions of the importance of the planning function: from those who view planning as
irrelevant and disruptive to those who view it as vital to their success. It is significant to note that some managers who are initially
skeptical about the worth of systematic planning are often transformed into strong advocates. They eventually "see the light."

In a similar fashion, we can observe large differences among organizations with regard to their degree of commitment to systematic planning. It appears to me that many organizations pass through four distinct phases: (1) anti-planning, (2) viewing planning as an "academic exercise," (3) piecemeal planning, and (4) integrated planning.

In the *anti-planning* phase, large numbers of managers within the organization strongly oppose systematic planning. We have heard their protests: "There is too much uncertainty in our field to allow us to plan." . . . "If we can't even forecast what's likely to happen next week, how can you expect us to forecast into next year?" . . . "A written plan is likely to put us in a strait jacket and not give us the flexibility that we need." . . . "A plan is simply a wish list based upon tenuous assumptions." . . . "It's a waste of time to plan." . . . And so it goes.

Eventually, perhaps through strong pressure from above, many of these managers will go through an exercise of planning which they view as an *academic exercise*. This means that they are not really committed to the planning process but will go through it simply to get their bosses "off their backs." We know where these plans end up: in the bottom right drawer of the manager's desk never to be seen again.

Then we can witness the same managers as they pass through a phase of *piecemeal planning*. During this phase, the managers do take the planning process seriously, but they have not been taught how to carry out integrated planning. The following procedure is typical. First, the upper-level managers instruct their direct reports to prepare written plans for the coming year. Suggested outlines for the plans are provided. These direct reports then scurry off to meet with their people to develop the written plans for their organizational units. Just as the deadline approaches, these unit plans are submitted to an upper-level manager. This manager then reviews the individual unit plans, staples them together, prepares a cover memo, and submits the total package to the next-higher manager. Following this procedure, all of the unit plans are submitted, but without any effort to truly integrate the unit plans.

After several years of such piecemeal planning, these same managers begin to get educated in the planning process. Perhaps the education comes about through on-the-job training, through reading, through attending seminars, or through inviting in an outside consultant. Regardless of how it comes about, it is apparent that a maturation in knowledge of the planning process has occurred. During this phase, we find these managers engaging in genuine *integrated planning*. Now we observe them creating alternative scenarios of possible futures, generating practical strategies that will be responsive to each of the scenarios, evaluating the strategies on the basis of return-on-investment, and then combining the selected strategies into an integrated action plan. It's hard to imagine that these are the very same managers who were so opposed to systematic planning several years previously.

Without pausing to ponder why it takes some managers so long to move from phase 1 to phase 4 in this process, let's move on with the story.

It is important to appreciate that an integrated plan includes both the *what* and the *how*. The *what* is revealed in the vision, which gives us a picture of where we are going. The *how* is revealed in the strategies, which tell us how we will get there.

Many managers would agree that adopting appropriate strategies may very well be the most demanding part of planning. After giving due consideration to the vision, it is necessary to identify potential strategies for translating the vision into reality. Some strategies will be rejected, and some will be retained. Importantly, to have the greatest impact on the organization as a whole, some of the strategies will be combined. Finally, there is a commitment of resources.

Carrying out this process calls for high-level skills. And these skills are not acquired through osmosis, but they come about through study, experience, and hard work.

Even after all of the hard work that went into developing the strategies, it is possible that the total effort may not succeed. When put to the test of the "real world," it may be found that the management team has selected the wrong strategies. Thus, in addition to being hard work, adopting appropriate strategies is a *risk enterprise*.

Because of the importance of selecting appropriate strategies, the leader of the organizational unit for which the plan is being developed should serve as the architect for the total process. Developing appropriate strategies is not an activity that should be delegated to others. Nor is it an activity that should be carried out by the leader single-handedly. It is clearly an activity that calls for a team approach, with the leader serving as the general architect to guide the process.

THE PROBLEM OF ACTION WITHOUT STRATEGY

Suppose that you were flying on a commercial airliner and discovered that the captain had no strategy for getting the plane from its present location to its presumed destination. On the brighter side, suppose that you also learned that the crew was healthy and in good spirits, the plane was in top-notch shape, and there was plenty of fuel. Even so, without the strategy, you would be a bit nervous, to say the least.

In the paper, "How to Evaluate Corporate Strategy," Seymour Tilles makes special note of the problem of action without strategy:

> No good military officer would undertake even a small-scale attack on a limited objective without a clear concept of strategy. No seasoned politician would undertake a campaign for a major office without an equally clear concept of his strategy. In the field of business management, however, we frequently find managers deploying resources on a large scale without any clear notion of what their strategy is.

I believe that Tilles is fairly accurate in his assessment of the present situation. Many managers work diligently at their jobs without the guidance of a strategy. A manager's actions, taken individually, may be clear and exacting but, taken collectively, are found lacking in unity and purpose.

The consequences of action without strategy are not good. Some of the undesirable results are summarized here.

A great deal of undirected activity. Without a clear definition of strategy, we find a considerable amount of aimless behavior. Perhaps the actions themselves are hard-hitting, but they are undirected. Under these circumstances, it is very easy for people to get caught up in the Activity Trap. They become engrossed in various activities simply for their own sake; there is no higher purpose than the activity itself. When enmeshed within such a quagmire, one may not fully appreciate the folly of the undirected activity. But an outside observer, looking at this aimless activity in a dispassionate manner, may be inclined to ask, "What is it all about?"

Lack of coordination across organizational units. Some managers fail to appreciate the basic Gestalt principle that the whole is greater than the sum of its parts. Indeed, each individual unit can create or produce a certain amount. But if the various units were well coordinated, it might be possible to create or produce twice or even three times that amount. Without the benefit of a clear strategy, it is impossible for the various units to coordinate their efforts. We may find piecemeal planning, but there will be no integrated planning. As a consequence, the potential, which might have been forthcoming from a unified effort, will go unrealized.

Crisis management. Lack of clear strategy leads to crisis management. And experience shows that crisis management produces excessive employee stress. A moderate amount of stress is not necessarily bad, but excessive stress is counterproductive. Yet, even with this generally accepted knowledge, we still find many managers heavily involved in crisis management. One crisis is dealt with, and the manager then moves on to attack the next one. It seems that some managers thrive on crises. In fact, it is not unreasonable to assume that some managers even *create* crises so that they can demonstrate their superior problem-solving abilities.

Lack of confidence in management. The security need is a basic need for the majority of employees. Having confidence in management, a confidence that upper-level managers know what they are doing and that they have a game plan for moving the organization toward its goals, is one way that this need can be met. Whenever employees discover that upper management has no well thought out strategy, they lose confidence. The security need is unfulfilled.

Low employee motivation and morale. When employees discover that management has no well thought out strategy, their motivation and morale will surely suffer. If management doesn't "have its act together," why should they themselves bother? Employees have a right to expect competent management. If such management is not evident, then the employees cannot be expected to put forth their best efforts to achieve the organizational goals.

Inefficient use of resources. I am familiar with a firm that has considerable duplication of facilities and equipment across its several divisions. This is a costly and inefficient situation. The duplication has come about because of a lack of overall strategy to guide the organization's efforts. Here we can witness piecemeal planning in operation: Each division develops its own plans without any coordination with the other divisions. It is hard to imagine the amount of total savings that might result from the development of a well coordinated strategy across the several divisions.

Low productivity. In simplistic terms, productivity usually is defined in terms of an input-output ratio. The input includes people, facilities, materials, money, and time. The output is defined in terms of the results achieved. In converting inputs into outputs, it is useful to view strategy as the "transfer function." Obviously, the quality of the transfer function will influence the organization's effectiveness and efficiency in its use of resources. The better the transfer function, the better the use of the resources, and in turn, the better the productivity.

In addition to these undesirable consequences of action without strategy, there is one more possible outcome: *you may end up someplace where you don't want to be.*

With such undesirable consequences as these, why do we find lack of well thought out strategy in business management? There may be a number of reasons, but I believe that one possible answer is that the planning function is quite different from the other management functions.

On a number of occasions, I have asked managers about the amount of time they spend in planning. Here there are two interrelated questions: (1) How much time *do you actually spend* in planning? and (2) How much time do you think you *should* spend in planning? Invariably, most managers respond that they spend much less time in planning than they should. Upon further inquiry, these managers acknowledge that they are unable to devote adequate time to planning because they are spending too much time "putting out fires" and "fighting alligators." Then, perhaps somewhat sheepishly, they admit that they are spending an enormous amount of time coping with fires and alligators *because they are lacking a systematic plan.* And so it goes.

It seems to me that many managers derive greater satisfaction from coping with fires and alligators than they do from planning. The former involves action; it is clearly results-oriented. Planning, on the other hand, is a cerebral activity that may or may not be results-producing. It involves sitting at your desk (or driving in your car) and creating possible scenarios of the future. Rather than *actual doing*, planning is *hard thinking.* Planning is simply a different type of activity than the other functions of management. I believe that this is a major part of the problem, but it is not an insurmountable problem.

In sum, I hope that you are persuaded that systematic planning is a vital part of your job as a manager. You should be aware of the negative consequences of action without strategy. Conversely, you should be aware of the positive consequences of action *with* strategy. Thus, for every manager who aspires to be an effective leader-manager, there is a clear challenge: Convert your vision into reality through well thought out strategy.

THE ESSENCE OF STRATEGY

In *Beyond the Quick Fix*, Ralph Kilman offers us a definition of strategy:

> Strategy is the way the organization positions itself in its setting in relation to its stakeholders given the organization's resources, capabilities, and mission. The strategy can be broken down further into specific objectives, policies, and plans as guides to all decisions and actions. [p. 38]

This definition suggests several key elements of strategy:

1. Understanding the mission: What is our business?
2. Determination of the needs and expectations of the stakeholders: What are the needs and expectations of our customers, our employees, and our stockholders?
3. Analysis of resources: What resources do we presently have and what resources do we need to achieve our mission and satisfy the needs and expectations of the stakeholders?
4. Analysis of capabilities: What capabilities do we presently have and what capabilities do we need to achieve our mission and the satisfy the needs and expectations of our stakeholders?
5. Positioning the organization: In the light of the above, what is our niche in the marketplace?
6. Development of an action plan: What specific sequence of actions should be carried out to translate our vision into reality?

James Brian Quinn, in *Strategies for Change*, elucidates the value of strategy:

> A well formulated strategy helps to marshal and allocate an organization's resources into a unique and viable posture based on its relative internal competencies and shortcom-

ings, anticipated changes in the environment, and con-
tingent moves by intelligent opponents. [p. 7]

Quinn goes on to stress that strategy is designed to deal with the
unknowable:

> Strategy deals not just with the unpredictable but also with
> the *unknowable*. For major enterprise strategies, no analyst
> could predict the precise ways in which all impinging forces
> could interact with each other, be distorted by nature or
> human emotions, or be modified by the imaginations and
> purposeful counteractions of intelligent opponents. Con-
> sequently, the essence of strategy is to *build a posture* that
> is so strong (and potentially flexible) in selective ways that
> the organization can achieve its goals despite the unfore-
> seeable ways external forces may actually interact when
> the time comes. [p. 163]

Building on the above ideas, we can now state the essence of
strategy:

> Strategy is the way the organization positions itself in order
> to be successful in translating its vision into reality.

To illustrate the notion of positioning, we can borrow an example used by Bennis and Nanus in their book, *Leaders*. An automobile
company might map its products as shown in Figure 16. Within this
framework, upper management should address itself to such questions as these: (1) What are the mission and goals of our organization? (2) What are our basic values? (3) What are the expectations
of our stakeholders? (4) What are our distinguishing resources and
capabilities? (5) What is our distinctive niche in the marketplace?
and (6) What is our plan of action?

This illustration is typical of what most people think of whenever
mention is made of positioning, namely, finding a niche for a product in the marketplace. It is important to appreciate that positioning applies to every department within the organization. This includes marketing, R&D, engineering, manufacturing, quality assurance, information systems, accounting and finance, human resources,
and all of the rest.

As an illustration of the generality of the concept of positioning,
let's consider the change in strategy of an accounting and finance
department in an enterprise with which I am familiar. This particular department was a vital part of a firm that is located in one

of the Arab nations, but the point to be made could apply to any type of organization in any part of the world.

During the early years of the life of this organization, the accounting and finance department had operated in a highly centralized manner. All of the people in the department were located on the fifth floor of the General Administration Building. The department's stated purpose was to regulate and control the financial matters of the entire organization. Essentially, this was an auditing function, and many of the staff members throughout the organization frequently complained that they felt that "Big Brother" was looking over their shoulders.

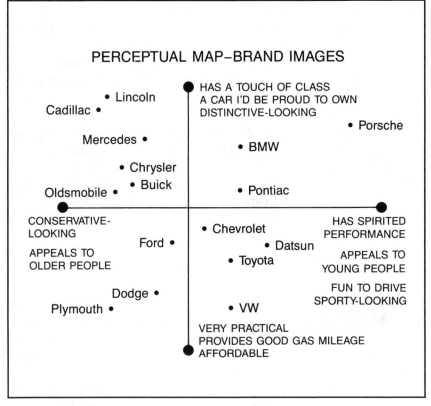

Source: Chrysler Corporation in the *Wall Street Journal*, March 22, 1984, p. 35.

Figure 16.   Product positioning in the automobile industry.

Later, to be more responsive to the needs of the operating departments, the mission and organizational structure of the accounting and finance department were altered substantially. The new mission called for the department to be a *service group* to all of the operating departments. Instead of viewing themselves as auditors, the accounting and financial people began to view themselves as "facilitators." In line with this change in mission, the organizational structure was changed to allow one of the members of the department to be assigned to each operating department as a business manager. Each of these business managers was to report to two supervisors: the manager of the operating department and the manager of business managers. This dual reporting relationship satisfied a twofold requirement: (1) responsiveness to the needs of the individual operating departments and (2) assurance of uniformity of policies and procedures throughout the organization.

From all reports, the new strategy was far superior to the old one, both in terms of the attitudes of the general staff and in terms of getting the job done in an effective and efficient manner. Thus, to be more responsive to the needs of its clients, the accounting and finance department's strategy was *to position itself differently*. And it was successful in doing so!

Indeed, strategy and positioning are important considerations for every manager within the organization, both vertically and horizontally. Every manager should have a clear vision for his or her unit and be able to translate the vision into reality through effective strategy. Strategy is the bridge between the vision and implementation. It is the transfer function.

ATTRIBUTES OF EFFECTIVE STRATEGY

The principal criterion in evaluating strategy is its utility as a transfer function: Is the strategy effective in translating inputs into outputs? This question is then followed by a second: What are the attributes of effective strategy? Certainly there are salient characteristics that make some strategies better than others.

Effective strategy has five key attributes: (1) responsiveness, (2) focus, (3) coherence, (4) flexibility, and (5) commitment. We will consider these attributes in the light of the wisdom provided by several different leaders in management thought.

1. Responsiveness

In his classic book, *Management*, Peter Drucker highlights the importance of responsiveness:

> With respect to the definition of business purpose and business mission, there is only one such focus, one starting point. It is the customer. The customer defines the business. The final question needed to come to grips with business purpose and business mission is: "What is value to the customer?" [p. 79]

It is important to appreciate that everyone has customers, those to whom we provide goods or services. For many of the operating departments, the customers are found outside of the organization. For most of the support departments, the customers are found within the operating departments. Thus, all managers should address themselves to Drucker's question: "What is value to the customer?" We know that any answer today might be obsolete in the near future. Thus, it is essential that you stay abreast of the changing needs and expectations of your customers both inside and outside the organization. Your strategy should then be designed to be responsive to those needs and expectations.

2. Focus

In the same book as the above, Drucker stresses the value of focus:

> No business can do everything. Even if it has the money, it will never have enough good people. It has to set priorities. The worst thing is to try to do a little bit of everything. This makes sure that nothing is accomplished. It is better to pick the wrong priority than none at all. [p. 119]

For many managers, it is difficult to focus, to concentrate the strategy on selected areas. Concentration means that some areas must be rejected, and what entrepreneur wants to reject anything? But reject we must. The effective leader-manager has a strong desire to achieve a reputation for excellence. Because of limitations in people, facilities, money, and time, it is impossible to achieve excellence in everything. Thus, it is essential to select particular areas on which to focus and then build the capabilities for achieving excellence in those selected

areas. In most situations, it is far better to achieve a reputation for being a "center of excellence" than for being a "jack-
of-all-trades."

3. Coherence

James Brian Quinn, in *Strategies for Change*, lays out an approach for achieving coherence:

> How can strategic coordination be achieved in a large
> enterprise? Conceptually, one can envision the prin-
> cipal thrusts — comprising the major elements of the
> strategy — as a matrix of coordinating plans laid out
> across the functional and operating units that must
> carry them out. Within its own plans and budgets, each
> division must provide *sufficient* support for each
> strategic thrust and make sure that the thrust is effec-
> tively implemented. As anyone knows who has tried
> it, this is a most difficult task in both an intellectual
> and a political sense. [p. 186]

An illustration of Quinn's proposal for achieving coherence
in the strategy is shown in Figure 17. Note that the vertical structure in the diagram represents the divisions of the functional
organization, and the horizontal structure represents the principal thrusts for the enterprise. The cross-hatched areas at the
intersections then represent the expected contribution of each division to each strategic thrust. Such an approach to aligning the
principal thrusts and the operating divisions will help provide
coherence in the development of overall strategy. Achieving this
type of coherence is no easy task, either intellectually or political-
ly, but this approach will prove to be far superior to a piecemeal
approach whereby each division goes its separate way in developing its own strategy.

4. Flexibility

In the paper, "Can Strategic Planning Pay Off?" Louis
Gerstner emphasizes the importance of flexibility:

> Most companies with active planning programs recog-
> nize the value of asking "what if" questions, taking
> important contingencies into account. Yet few really
> address the issue in a substantive way. A frequent ex-
> cuse is that there are so many potential contingencies

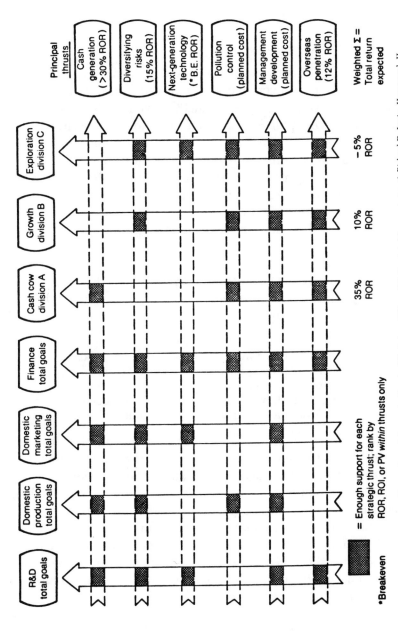

Figure 17.   A matrix of thrusts for a chemical specialties company.

From *Strategies for Change: Logical Incrementalism*, by J.B. Quinn, 1980, p. 187. Reprinted by permission of Richard D. Irwin, Homewood, IL.

that it would take years to analyze them all. The
obvious answer to this objection is that one can
and should be very selective, and deal only with
the one or two possible contingencies that could
upset the entire strategy.

No manager has the foresight to predict exactly what will happen five, three, or even one year into the future. Some would
contend that we cannot even predict the events of tomorrow. For
this reason, every plan is based on assumptions, suppositions that
particular events are likely to occur. These assumptions can be
categorized as optimistic, pessimistic, or most likely. The effective leader-manager develops strategy along these lines. The most
likely scenario of the future is clearly laid out, but this is backed
up with an optimistic and a pessimistic scenario. Alternative
strategies are then developed accordingly.

5. Commitment

In the paper, "The Future as the Basis for Establishing a
Shared Culture," Margaret Mead makes special note of the importance of commitment:

> But always the surest guarantee of change and growth
> is the inclusion of living persons in every stage of an
> activity. Their lives, their experience, and their contin-
> uing response — even their resistances — infuse with life
> any plan which, if living participants are excluded, lies
> on the drawing board and loses its reality.

We frequently find elegant plans "lying on the drawing
board." Even though the plans may satisfy the four requirements
of responsiveness, focus, coherence, and flexibility, they still may
be stored in the lower right hand drawer of the manager's desk
never to be seen again. Satisfying the first four requirements is
necessary but not sufficient. Achieving sufficiency requires the
satisfaction of a fifth criterion: commitment. Here we mean commitment by those people who are expected to implement the
plans. The key to getting this commitment is *to actively involve
the implementers in the planning process.*

Thus, most experts on the subject would agree that effective
strategy is characterized by these factors: responsiveness, focus, co-

herence, flexibility, and commitment. A strategy distinguished by all five is likely to succeed, but the absence of any one of them should be reason for concern. As you participate in the development of strategy, make certain that you give due consideration to all five factors.

ON DEVELOPING STRATEGY

The effective leader-manager knows that planning can and should be carried out in a systematic manner. It is not a "seat-of-the-pants" activity. The plan is a bridge from where we are to where we want to be. To get to "where we want to be," it is essential that the bridge be robust.

A systematic approach to planning is shown in Figure 18. The principal theme here is a "participative systems approach" to planning. It is a *systems* approach in that it is an integration of inter-related activities directed toward common goals. It is a *participative* approach in that it is intended to involve every member of the management team. This participative systems approach may be applied to the enterprise as a whole or to any unit within the enterprise. The 10-step process is summarized here:

1. **Establish Planning Task Force**

    A planning task force should be established to guide and coordinate the entire planning process. If the plan is being developed for the enterprise as a whole, then the task force would be comprised of the chief executive officer and all of the persons reporting directly to the CEO. If the plan is being developed for a division of the enterprise, then the task force would be comprised of the division head and all of the persons reporting directly to the division head. And so on. It is assumed that the senior manager on each task force would serve as the task force leader.

    At the outset, it is important that the task force leader conduct an orientation session with all of the team members. Included in this session should be a review and discussion of the team's goals, the roles and responsibilities of the team members, the decision-making process, the time schedule, and any other relevant information. At the end of this session, it should be clear to all members

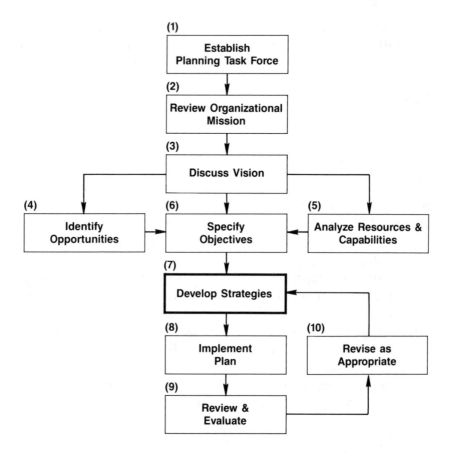

Figure 18.   A systematic approach to planning.

where they are going in the planning process and how they plan to get there.

2. Review Organizational Mission

The starting point of the planning process is a review of the organizational mission. The mission is a single statement regarding the organization's reason for existence, or as Drucker would say, "What is our business?" For Battelle, the mission is the advancement and utilization of science for the benefit of humankind. For AT&T, the stated mission is to provide quality communication systems to people anyplace in the world at a reasonable price.

Perhaps the mission is already clear to all members of the team, but if it exists without having been communicated clearly, then it should be communicated. If a mission statement does not exist, then it should be formulated.

3. Discuss Vision

The leader should present to the task force his or her vision — the desired future state of the organization.* This vision is an outline of a dream: a scenario of what the organization might become. The team members would be requested to react to the statement of vision: to agree, to disagree, to debate, but above all, to be honest in expressing their views.

With the leader serving as the architect in constructing the vision, as well as the conciliator in conducting the meeting, the team members would be expected to serve as the builders in completing the construction. The end result of this step should be an embellished vision that all team members will actively support.

4. Identify Opportunities

In considering opportunities, the task force must address these fundamental questions: In the light of the vision, what are the present and future opportunities for the organization? What opportunities are we presently pursuing? What are the new opportunities that we *should* be pursuing?

One obvious source for obtaining answers to these questions is the customer, both existing customers and potential customers. It is essential to survey the needs of these customers and develop products or services that are responsive to their needs. The two critical skills called for here are the ability to ask good questions and the ability to listen.

5. Analyze Resources and Capabilities

The next step involves an orderly assessment of the organization's strengths and weaknesses. With the identification of opportunities having been accomplished, we now consider in detail the organization's resources and capabilities for taking advantage of these opportunities.

Here is a practical technique for making this assessment. First,

---

*As used here, "organization" refers to either the enterprise as a whole or to any unit within the enterprise.

construct a two-way table in which the identified opportunities are listed along one side and the resources and capabilities needed for taking advantage of these opportunities are listed along the other side. Then, on a 1-to-10 scale, evaluate each of your organization's resources and capabilities in terms of its merit in contributing to the identified opportunities. A careful examination of the resulting data should help you answer these questions: What are our present strengths? What are our present weaknesses? What resources and capabilities should we develop?

6. Specify Objectives

The next step in the process is to formulate clear objectives for the coming year. These objectives should be a clear statement of intent, what the organization aspires to accomplish. The objectives should focus on the critical success factors: those factors that are most likely to determine the overall success of the organization.

Translating goals into objectives is a skillful art. While goals are general, objectives are specific. A key criterion for an objective is "verifiability": Any two persons observing the outcome would agree whether or not the objective was achieved. In addition to being verifiable, the set of objectives should be comprehensive, challenging, and consistent with anticipated resources.

7. Develop Strategies

The development of strategies is the most important step in the entire planning process. With the objectives specifying *what* is to be achieved, the strategies specify *how* the objectives are to be achieved. As indicated previously, the strategies should satisfy these five criteria: responsiveness, focus, coherence, flexibility, and commitment.

In *Business Policy*, C. Roland Christensen and his associates offer a useful check list for evaluating strategy. It is suggested that the planning task force evaluate its preliminary formulation of strategies in the light of the questions presented in Figure 19. In addition to these nine questions, I would add a tenth: Have alternative or contingency strategies been adequately developed?

8. Implement Plan

Completing all of the steps up to this point is a futile exercise

1. Is the strategy identifiable and has it been made clear either in words or practice?

2. Does the strategy take advantage of perceived opportunity?

3. Is the strategy consistent with corporate competence and resources, both present and projected?

4. Are the major provisions of the strategy and the program of major policies of which it is comprised internally consistent?

5. Is the chosen level of risk feasible in economic and personal terms?

6. Is the strategy appropriate to the personal values and aspirations of the key managers?

7. Is the strategy appropriate to the desired level of contribution to society?

8. Does the strategy constitute a clear stimulus to organizational effort and commitment?

9. Are there early indications of the responsiveness of markets and market segments to the strategy?

From *Business Policy: Text and Cases*, by C.R. Christensen, K.R. Andrews, and J.L. Bower, 1978, p. 136–139. Reprinted by permission of Richard D. Irwin, Homewood, IL.

Figure 19. The evaluation of strategy.

if it does not lead to implementation. Here we move from the world of cognition and cerebral activity to that of action. These are two different worlds, and they call for different consideration.

One of the keys to the successful implementation of the plan is to specify clearly the accountabilities. It is essential that the individual managers be given responsibility for, and be held accountable for, implementing the various aspects of the plan. Make certain that no objective or required action is left uncovered. Without a clear explanation of the accountabilities, the written plan may very well remain hidden in the lower right hand drawer of the manager's desk.

9. Review and Evaluate

It is important that the plan be reviewed and evaluated during the period of implementation. Perhaps quarterly, the management team should meet to discuss these questions: (1) What has been accomplished during the last operating period? (2) What problems and opportunities have been encountered? (3) What is being done to deal with these problems and opportunities? and (4) What specific actions are planned for the next review period?

With the ever-demanding pressures of day-to-day activities, there may be a tendency for managers to place the plan on a "back burner." Many other demands are given higher priority. But if accountabilities for implementing the plan are clearly delineated and review dates are established, managers are much more likely to keep the plan on the "front burner."

10. Revise as Appropriate

Planning should be viewed as a dynamic process. Strategies, for example, should be looked upon as heuristic guidelines rather than as algorithms. This means that strategies should be viewed as guidelines for action rather than as rigid cookbooks for action. Certainly there should be specifics in the plan with regard to objectives, action sequences, and budgets, but these specifics should be amenable to modification in the light of changing realities. The plan should not be cast in concrete. It should be revised as appropriate.

As mentioned previously, the key criterion in evaluating strategy is whether it helps convert the vision into reality. Does the strategy help the unit move from its previous state to the desired state? Thus, the real test of a strategy is not in the beauty and elegance of the written plan, but simply, "Does it bear fruit?"

This participative systems approach is an effective planning strategy. If carried out according to the guidelines presented here, it should bear fruit. But it is not an easy process. It requires *high-level* thinking and *prolonged* thinking. Further, it requires a substantial commitment of time. There are certain to be problems and frustrations encountered along the way. We would expect, however, that the headaches encountered would be more than offset by the accrued benefits.

BENEFITS OF A CLEAR STRATEGY

Assuming that the proposed approach to planning is carried out successfully, what are the expected benefits?

Focusing of action on purposes. Clear strategy can focus action on purposes. Without a road map, who knows where the participants might end up? With the existence of a clear road map, and one that has been communicated to all persons involved, it is very likely that the participants will end up where they want to be.

Better coordination across organizational units. Clear strategy can help achieve coordination across organizational units. There can be a sharing of common objectives and resources to the end of achieving the objectives. This sharing can benefit everyone involved, both in terms of effectiveness and efficiency. The end result should be a testimony to the notion that the whole is greater than the sum of its parts.

More proactive management. Without clear strategy, managers get caught up in reactive management. In a helter-skelter environment, the managers simply run from one crisis to another. The establishment of clear strategy should help turn this situation around. Instead of "fighting alligators" and "putting out fires," managers should be able to spend more time constructing alligator cages and developing fire-prevention programs. There will still be a need for a certain amount of reactive management, but this should take a back seat to proactive management.

Greater confidence in management. Without the existence of clear strategy, we cannot expect the staff to have confidence in management. But if managers can demonstrate to the staff that they know where they are going and how they plan to get there, they will surely instill confidence in their people. This particular action will help meet the security needs of all staff.

Higher employee motivation and morale. The lack of clear strategy will have a debilitating effect on employee motivation and morale. But if well thought out strategy is communicated to the staff — and it makes sense to them — their motivation and morale will be enhanced. The employees will feel better about their jobs and will have a stronger desire to perform well at their jobs.

Better use of resources. The key idea behind strategy is to make good use of resources to the end of achieving the organizational objectives. Here we are not talking about incremental improvements; we are talking about orders of magnitude.

Higher productivity. The establishment of clear strategy can help convert an unproductive organization into a productive one. As mentioned previously, strategy may be viewed as the transfer function for converting inputs into outputs, resources into achievements. The better the transfer function, the better the use of resources, and in turn, the better the productivity.

These are significant benefits. They can easily spell the difference between success and failure for either the enterprise as a whole or a particular unit within the enterprise. Importantly, the establishment of clear strategy will help convert the vision into reality. That is what leadership is all about!

VII

Communicating

The fundamental fact of human existence is neither the individual as such nor the aggregate as such. What is peculiarly characteristic of the human world is above all that something takes place between one being and another the like of which can be found nowhere in nature.

Martin Buber
Between Man and Man

The Life of Dialogue • Interpersonal Communication • Written Communication • Oral Presentations • Meetings • Organizational Communication

---

THE LIFE OF DIALOGUE

In the course of conducting management seminars, I have had occasion to ask the participants to describe the best leader they have ever known, and especially: What leader has had the greatest impact on your life? A number of different leadership traits are mentioned, but frequently I hear these two: "honesty" and "ability to communicate." Combining these two traits gives us "an honest communicator."

Most people want to work for an honest communicator. In the descriptions of their favorite leaders, I hear such statement as these: "He's very much up-front with everybody." . . . "She tells it like it really is." . . . "He has no hidden agendas." . . . "You always know where she's coming from." The common theme is evident.

Why is there so much focus placed on the importance of honest communication? Perhaps because it is so rare.

Martin Buber, in *Pointing the Way*, highlights one of the major problems of the day:

> That peoples can no longer carry on authentic dialogue with one another is not only the most acute symptom of the pathology of our time, it is also that which most urgently makes a demand of us. [p. 238]

This observation by Buber is echoed by Clark Moustakas in his book, *Loneliness and Love*:

> Increasingly, I have become painfully aware of the terribleness of most communication: of people talking but not saying what they mean; of the contradiction between the outward words and expressions and the inner meanings and messages; of people looking as if they were listening without any real connection or contact with one another. [p. 130]

The problem focused on by both Buber and Moustakas is the lack of authentic dialogue between human persons. People talk, but they don't say what they mean. People talk, but they don't express their inner thoughts and feelings. People talk, but they don't listen. Even though these people are using familiar words, there obviously is something seriously amiss in the communication.

Some insight into what is amiss can be gleaned by considering Buber's formulation of three different types of communication. First, there is monologue: one-way communication in which there is a sender but no receiver. Second, there is technical communication: two-way communication which involves the exchange of data and information. And third, there is dialogue: honest communication with the intention of establishing a living mutual relation. Unfortunately, the prevailing forms of communication in many organizations are monologue and technical communication. We see few instances of authentic dialogue.

The meaning of dialogue has been elucidated by Emil Fackenheim in *The Philosophy of Martin Buber*,* in which he contrasts the I-It relation and the I-Thou relation. He notes:

> While the I-It relation is necessarily abstract, the I-Thou relationship cannot be abstract. The partners communicate

---

*Edited by Paul Arthur Schilpp and Maurice Friedman.

not this or that, but themselves; that is, they must *be in* the communication. Further — since the relation of dialogue is mutual — they must be in a state of openness to the other, that is, to *this* other at *this* time and in *this* place. Hence both the I and the Thou of every genuine dialogue are irreplaceable. Every dialogue is unique. [p. 279]

The meaning of dialogue can be understood by considering it in the light of its polar opposite: Machiavellianism. The well-known political writer of the sixteenth century, Machiavelli, proposed to the Prince a form of communication that is shrouded in insincerity and deception. Its intention is manipulation. Dialogue, on the other hand, is grounded in sincerity and honesty. Its intention is the establishment of a living mutual relation. In these two forms of communication, both the ends and means are radically different. Moreover, the outcomes are radically different!

The principal requirement for dialogue is authenticity. By authenticity is meant a congruence between the inner and the outer. Everyone carries these two selves: the inner self, which is known only to the possessor, and the outer self, which is witnessed by others. We can say that a person is authentic to the extent that these two selves are in harmony. In the words of Abraham Maslow: "Phoniness is reduced toward the zero point." The *sine qua non* for dialogue is authenticity.

Whenever I mention the importance of authenticity in leadership seminars, I usually can expect at least one participant to raise this question: "But isn't there a certain amount of risk involved in being authentic? Wouldn't I be exposing myself?" The answer is "yes," but I believe that the effective leader-manager prefers to deal with these risks as they arise — and perhaps experience a few bruises along the way — rather than to sacrifice his or her selfhood. It's simply a matter of priorities.

The effective leader-manager makes a commitment to authentic dialogue in all forms of communication. These various forms of communication are shown in the "Wheel of Communication" of Figure 20. Included are these components: a hub that represents a commitment to a life of dialogue; four spokes that represent four specific forms of communication (interpersonal communication, written communication, oral presentations, and meetings); and a rim that represents organizational communication (the application of all forms of communication in carrying out the functions of management). With all components intact, the wheel should move forward; that is, the leader-manager should achieve credibility as an honest communicator.

Let's assume that the leader-manager makes a genuine commitment to a life of dialogue and manifests this commitment in all forms of communication. What is the expected outcome?

There are a number of possible desirable outcomes, but one in particular bears special mention: *trust*. Whenever we find lack of authentic dialogue in a work group, we usually find lack of trust. But when we do find authentic dialogue, we usually find trust. There is an obvious relation between the two.

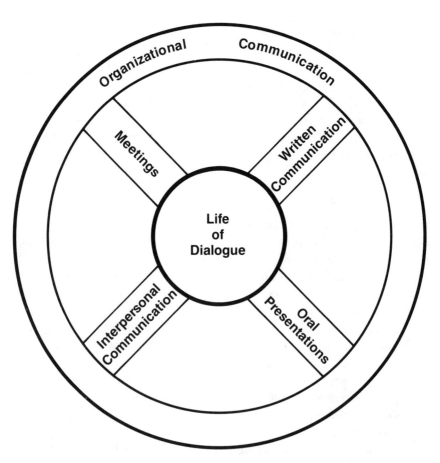

Figure 20.   Forms of communication.

Trust is the glue that holds the group together. Because leadership is a *relationship* between leader and followers, trust is essential for the execution of the leadership function. Without trust, all is lost, but with trust, we can expect great things to happen. This is what authentic dialogue is all about.

INTERPERSONAL COMMUNICATION

The leader-manager is expected to be effective in interpersonal communication. Throughout the day, the manager is communicating face to face on a one-to-one basis. This communication includes giving instructions, asking questions, answering questions, listening to concerns, making suggestions, and on and on. To the individual staff members, these exchanges may be either uplifting or depressing. Regardless of which way they go, we know that the exchanges can have a significant carry-over effect to other aspects of the job.

Because of its commonplace nature, interpersonal communication usually is taken for granted. We fail to appreciate the complexity and subtleties of what is transpiring. One person is attempting to translate some thoughts into verbal symbols; the receiver is attempting to understand the verbal symbols and integrate them into thought. In addition to the words themselves, tone of voice and body language serve as conveyors of information. Even when two persons are trying their best to communicate effectively, misunderstandings inevitably arise. Imagine how much the situation is confounded when one or both of the parties attempt to be somewhat deceptive or manipulative in the communication process.

A number of barriers are found in interpersonal communication, including not being "present," not listening, premature evaluation, the tendency to debate rather than search for truth, a win-lose attitude, and others. The effective leader-manager is aware of these barriers and attempts to overcome them.

The key to effective interpersonal communication is authentic dialogue. As mentioned previously, dialogue means open communication with the intention of establishing a living mutual relation. It includes both speaking and listening; it includes both the expression of thoughts and the expression of feelings. It is a mutual sharing between one self and another self.

With authentic dialogue serving as the hub, guidelines for effective interpersonal communication are presented.

1. **Express your thoughts clearly.** To be effective in interpersonal communication, organize your thoughts. Think through what you plan to say before you say it. Choose the appropriate words that will best communicate these thoughts, and speak in the language of the listener. Strive for utmost clarity.

2. **Be willing to express your feelings.** Those people who are able to express their feelings are more likely to be effective communicators than those who are not. This does not mean an irresponsible venting of emotions; rather, it means expression of feelings tempered with responsibility. If you are unable or unwilling to express your feelings, others may view you as bland. Your people want to know where you are coming from. Tell them! Move beyond merely exchanging data and information. Enrich your communication with a clear expression of your feelings about the issues at hand.

3. **Put yourself in the place of the other person.** The effective communicator has empathy: the capacity to participate in another's thoughts or feelings. Empathy is the ability to see the world through the other person's eyes. It is an attitude, a frame of mind, that has a profound effect on the quality of the communication. Empathy is what helps establish the exchange as a living mutual relation.

4. **Be "truly present."** When engaging in interpersonal communication, many managers appear to be preoccupied with other thoughts. Their body language conveys the impression that their thoughts are focused on something other than the matter at hand. Don't be guilty of this type of behavior. Whenever talking with another person, give that person your undivided attention. Even if you have only 10 minutes to give, give the person 10 minutes of your undivided attention. Be present.

5. **Be a good listener.** It has been estimated that no more than about 10 percent of the general population might be considered really good listeners. That means that about 90 percent of us have room for improvement. It will be to your credit if you develop a reputation for being a good listener. Be an active listener. Listen with

understanding. Ask good questions. Paraphrase the key points that the other person has made. Check your perception of the person's feelings. Link the elements. Achieve unity. These are things that you can learn to do. Great effort is required, but making the effort will surely enhance your effectiveness in interpersonal communication.

6. **Postpone evaluation.** Whenever a new idea is being presented for consideration, many managers are too quick on the draw in evaluating the idea. Before they have really understood the idea, they judge it to be either good or bad. Such behavior tends to inhibit communication and may cause the manager to miss out on some promising ideas. Whenever a new idea is being presented to you, discipline yourself to postpone evaluation until after you have demonstrated that you fully understand the idea.

7. **Avoid becoming hostile when another person's views differ from your own.** Employees learn a great deal about their manager on the basis of how the manager responds to opposing views. (And body language speaks louder than words.) If the manager appears threatened or distressed whenever an employee offers an opposing view, the employees in all likelihood will be reluctant to challenge the manager in the future. As a consequence, the manager's ideas may go untested, and some potentially good ideas may never be considered. Avoid becoming hostile to opposing views. Try to understand the other person's views: what they mean, how they came about, and why the person supports these particular views. Then, when appropriate, try to incorporate these views into your own thinking, while at the same time giving due credit to the person who generated the ideas.

8. **Be willing to change your convictions as new truths are uncovered.** Too many people believe that they have a "lock" on truth. There is only one way to the top of the mountain, and that is *their* way. Their own views are obviously correct, which means that any opposing views are obviously incorrect. One of the greatest challenges for you as a leader-manager is to keep an open mind. This does not mean a wishy-washy approach in which you agree with every opposing view, but it does mean that you will hear others out and try to understand their views — even when the views are contrary to your own. Perhaps it will turn out to be a significant

learning experience: You may glean some insights that will help you strengthen your own views.

9. **Be willing to confront.** Conflict is an integral part of life. If we are encouraging people to be authentic in expressing their thoughts and feelings, conflict is inevitable; if we are calling for people to be creative in expressing their own views, conflict is inevitable; and if we are requiring people to work in complex and ever-changing organizations that have competing demands, conflict is inevitable. Conflict is not something to be avoided; rather, it is something to be guided and channeled for productive ends. Whenever your views differ from those of others, be willing to confront. This is essential for authentic dialogue.

10. **Think win-win.** When confronting others, there are those who think only in terms of win-lose. There obviously will be a winner and a loser. This is a basic attitude that has been ingrained over the years. Don't get trapped in the win-lose mentality. Transcend it! Focus on ends rather than means. Ask yourself: In this particular confrontation, what might be done to assure that both my adversary and I achieve our objectives? How can we both emerge as winners?

WRITTEN COMMUNICATION

The leader-manager is expected to be an effective writer. Forms of written communication include memos, letters, minutes of meetings, proposals, and reports. The leader-manager must be able to convert his or her thoughts into readable form. In addition to achieving understanding on the part of the reader, the manager often is attempting to motivate the reader to take certain actions. Effective writing, that which produces results, is an essential skill for the manager.

A number of barriers are associated with written communication. The most common is lack of clarity: The reader simply does not understand what the writer is trying to say. Another is lack of focus: The diversity of ideas in the document prevents the reader from grasping the central message. Still another is dullness: The written material is uninteresting and boring. A concerted effort on the part of the manager, which includes planning the writing and rewriting preliminary drafts, can help overcome these barriers.

Even though written communication is different from interpersonal communication, the writer nevertheless can focus on dialogue. Establishing a living mutual relation through written communication is no easy task, but it can be done. It requires that you visualize your reader during the process of writing, to form a mental image of your reader sitting on the other side of your desk. Moreover, it requires that you put yourself into your writing—to write as though you are talking to the reader. Such an approach will help your writing come alive. It will read as though one living human being is addressing another living human being.

Here are some practical guidelines for effective writing.

1. **Write in the language of the reader.** More than 2,000 years ago Aristotle suggested that, "When talking to the carpenter, use the language of the carpenter." This bit of advice is as valid today as it was then. Before you begin the writing, think about the reader. Reflect on the person's education, experience, and interests. Then write accordingly.

2. **Focus on the key idea.** Whether it is a one-page memo or a 20-page report, your written material should have one central idea. Perhaps there are a number of secondary and tertiary ideas, but these should be in support of the main idea. In planning your writing, give attention to the one principal idea that you want to convey to your reader audience. Then organize the entire document to support this idea. This will give your document *unity*—it will be all of a piece.

3. **Organize your material in a coherent manner.** Readers will understand your material better if it is organized in "chunks." According to the information scientists, the maximum number of chunks that most people can grasp is seven; for many kinds of writing, however, the number of chunks, or major points, should be limited to three or four. These major chunks can then be subdivided into smaller chunks. Once you have identified the major points and the supporting points, arrange them in a logical order. Here is where you will realize the importance of outlining the material before you begin the actual writing. This will give your document *coherence*: there will be a logical flow.

4. **Choose a style and stick to it.** It is important to appreciate that

your style of writing will have an impact on the reader and may communicate as much as the content. The style is your mode of expressing your thoughts in language; it is your tone. Style includes choice of words, sentences, and paragraph format. It should be appropriate to the situation and to the parties involved. The important thing is to select an appropriate style and stick to it.

5. **Make the paragraph the basic unit of composition.** If you can write a good paragraph, then you have mastered an important part of writing. The paragraph should hold together: it should be all of a piece. Typically, each paragraph should contain one idea. This idea is reflected in the first sentence of the paragraph, the topic sentence. As you write the paragraph, you are developing the idea. The next step is to then connect the paragraphs through good transition sentences.

6. **Use definite, specific, concrete language.** Story has it that a man wrote to an insurance company in search of his long-lost cousin. He knew that his cousin at one time had a life insurance policy with this company and thus thought that the company might know his whereabouts. The man's initial letter of inquiry brought this reply: "We are sorry to inform you that your long-lost cousin failed to achieve the expectations delineated in the actuarial tables." The man wrote back with the question: "What does your letter mean?" And this was the reply: "He's dead."

7. **Use the active voice rather than the passive voice.** The active voice has more impact — more punch — than the passive voice. Grammatically, this sentence written in the passive voice is acceptable: "My first visit to Geneva will always be remembered by me." But much better is one written in the active voice: "I shall always remember my first visit to Geneva." Rather than say, "I was in receipt of your letter," you should say, "I received your letter."

8. **Use short words rather than long words.** I once read a technical report that contained the word "utilized" four times on one page. My thought was, Why didn't the writer select the word "use" rather than "utilize"? It seems that some writers choose the longer words just to impress others. But you will find that the really expert writers choose short words because they have more punch. They carry their meaning quickly. Certainly long technical words

must be used sometimes simply because they are the only appropriate words. When selecting the nontechnical words, however, choose short ones.

9. **Omit needless words.** Writing should be specific and to the point. Unless a word makes a contribution, omit it. Rather than say "She is a woman who," say "She." Rather than say "The fact that he had succeeded," say "His success." Rather than say "a rather important point," say "an important point." Rather than say "It is logical and coherent," say "It is coherent." Scrutinize your draft material and omit needless words.

10. **Apply the basic rules of grammar properly.** Some years ago the Dean of Engineering in a large state-supported university was criticized because the curriculum for engineering students did not include a course in grammar. His reply was published as a headline in the school newspaper: UNIVERSITY DEAN CLAIMS THAT ENGINEERING STUDENTS DON'T NEED NO GRAMMAR. Engineering students do need to know grammar. And certainly every leader-manager needs to know grammar. If you would like to brush up on the rules of grammar, I recommend the excellent book, *The Elements of Style*, by William Strunk and E. B. White.

ORAL PRESENTATIONS

The leader-manager is expected to be able to give effective oral presentations. Many situations in the workplace call for the manager to stand before a group of people and deliver a presentation. This may be for the manager's staff, for other managers, for clients, or for any other group of people. It is clear that oral presentations give the manager considerable visibility and an opportunity to have an impact on others. Hence, the ability to give an effective oral presentation is an essential skill for every manager.

A number of barriers are associated with oral presentations. These barriers may be grouped into three phases of the presentation: (1) preparation, (2) delivery, and (3) evaluation. With regard to preparation, common problems are lack of clear definition of purpose and lack of organization. With regard to delivery, common problems are failure to address the audience, lack of enthusiasm on the part of the speaker, and poor visual aids. With respect to evaluation, a common problem is not being sensitive to the feedback given by the audience during the presentation. Any manager who desires to be an effective speaker should be able to overcome these barriers.

The key to effective oral presentations is authentic dialogue. When called on to deliver an oral presentation, some managers focus only on "covering the material." This is their mind-set: "There are 20 visuals; each visual will require about two minutes; thus, the entire presentation will require about 40 minutes. I should be careful in gauging my time." Standing in sharp contrast is the speaker who focuses on dialogue with the audience. This speaker has a different mind-set: "Who are the individual persons in the audience? What are their interests? What are their expectations? How can I best relate to them?" This is an attitude of "inclusion": including the audience in consciousness throughout the entire presentation. It is a radically different attitude than that which focuses only on "covering the material."

Some guidelines for effective oral presentations are presented here.

1. **Suit the speech to the audience.** A good speech is always designed for a particular group of listeners at a particular time. The beginning point in preparing your speech should be to find out all you can about the audience. What are their interests? What are their expectations? Why are they attending the presentation? Do your homework in obtaining answers to these questions. Then tailor your presentation accordingly. Whenever you find yourself in a situation in which you are unable to obtain this information before to the presentation, take a few minutes at the beginning of the session to find out about the particular interests of the audience.

2. **Determine your central idea.** A good oral presentation will have unity: a central idea will hold it together. There may be anywhere from four to seven major ideas that you want to get across, but they should all be in support of the central idea. This central idea may be the key feature of a product or service that you are promoting, the principal mission of an organization that you are describing, the major purpose of a project, or the chief recommendation of a study. Whatever it is, it should be clearly formulated in your mind and then set down on paper as the cornerstone of the entire presentation.

3. **Clearly define the purpose of the presentation.** Ask yourself this question: Why am I giving this presentation? You should think through exactly what you want the listeners to get from the speech. What do you want them to "have" at the end of the presentation? Perhaps you want them to *know something* that they do not now know. Perhaps you want them to have a *different attitude* about something. Or, perhaps you want them to *take certain actions*. Defining this purpose clearly in your mind will be valuable to you in developing a coherent presentation.

4. **Gather information from your own experience.** As you begin to gather information for your presentation, you have two possible sources: your own experience or the experience of others. I have observed that speakers usually are more alive and interesting if they are describing their own experiences. Certainly, you may want to include in your speech the ideas and works of others, but these should be treated as supplementary materials. Always begin with your own experiences and then add to these as appropriate.

5. **Organize the material in a coherent fashion.** A good speech has unity and coherence. This means that there is a central idea, and the idea is developed in a logical manner. This is the important question: What is logical *to your audience?* It may not be the same as the order in which you developed the idea. Put yourself in the place of the audience and then arrange your points in a sequence that will make sense to them. The same suggestion applies here as in writing: Break the presentation down into three to five major "chunks" and then sequence the chunks in a manner that will make the most sense to the audience.

6. **Prepare good visual aids.** Research on oral presentations demonstrates the value of good visual aids. It is clear that there will be greater audience retention if they both hear and see the information than if they are merely told or are merely shown the information. Prepare good visuals, and don't make the mistake of simply reading the visuals to the audience. They know how to read. The visuals should present highlights only, on which you should then elaborate. Finally, make certain that the visuals are a creditable representation of you and your organization.

7. **Speak from an outline.** Don't make the mistake of either attempt-

ing to memorize your speech or reading your speech. The first suffers from the possibility of your forgetting a segment and then not knowing what to say next. The second will cause the audience to lose interest and perhaps doze. In the majority of cases, it is best to speak from an outline. The outline, perhaps placed on a lectern in front of you, should cover your major points arranged in a logical order. You should then be able to merely glance at the outline and elaborate on each point while at the same time maintaining good eye contact with the audience.

8. **Let your feelings show.** You could have an excellent speech in terms of content and coherence, but the speech as a whole could still be a failure because of the delivery. To prevent this from happening, let your feelings show. Show your enthusiasm! Why are you interested in the topic? Why is the topic of interest to the audience? What are the implications of what you are presenting? What are some of the unresolved issues? Tell your audience! Do not limit your communication to mere words. Communnicate through your tone of voice and body language.

9. **Maintain good eye contact with the audience.** One of the greatest compliments you can pay an audience is to look at them. Assuming the audience is not too large, look at each person individually. Each member of the audience will then feel that you are addressing him or her personally. By speaking from an outline, you should be able to maintain good eye contact with each member of the audience. In addition to benefiting the audience, this mode of delivery will benefit you by giving needed feedback.

10. **Be flexible.** In many situations, you must be prepared to modify your presentation, during the presentation, based on the feedback you are receiving from the audience. On the basis of the facial expressions of members of the audience and the questions that are raised during the presentation, you should be obtaining a great deal of feedback regarding audience comprehension and interest. Use this information! Be prepared to adjust your presentation on the basis of the signals you are receiving. By demonstrating to your audience that you are able and willing to adjust your presentation to accommodate them, you will show them that you are a perceptive and sensitive human being rather than an automaton.

MEETINGS

The leader-manager is expected to be able to conduct productive meetings. We define a "meeting" as an assemblage of three or more persons working together face to face. The meeting may be with staff, with other managers, with clients, or with a combination of these parties. Managers may spend anywhere from 10% to 50% of their workday attending meetings. Thus, it is essential that the manager be able to conduct meetings that are both effective (they get results) and efficient (they are economical in use of time).

A number of barriers are associated with meetings. Large numbers of managers complain that many of the meetings they attend are unproductive. Here are some of the most common complaints: "The meeting had no focus." . . . "The basic problem was never really defined." . . . "There was much jumping from topic to topic." . . . "There was too much wheel spinning." . . . "One or two people dominated the meeting." . . . "We never achieved a sense of closure as to what would happen next." . . . "There was no follow-up." These are serious barriers. But all of them can be dealt with by any manager who wants to make a concerted effort to become a successful leader of meetings.

The key to conducting productive meetings is authentic dialogue. This means that the participants in the meeting are establishing living mutual relationships with one another. The participants are honest and open with each other. They feel free to express both their thoughts and feelings. And they listen to each other. The leader is the principal person who sets the tone and creates the climate for dialogue.

The following are guidelines for conducting productive meetings.

1. **Clearly define the purpose of the meeting.** Whenever you are scheduling a meeting, you should have a very clear idea about the meeting's purpose. You should ask yourself: Why are we having this meeting? Do we want to merely inform? Do we want to solve a problem? Do we want to make a decision? It is useful to phrase the question in this manner: What should the participants "have" at the end of the meeting that they do not now have? You should clearly define the purpose of the meeting in your own mind and then communicate the purpose to all of the participants.

2. **Prepare an agenda.** A common complaint about meetings is that

the leader was unable to keep the meeting "on track." In some cases, the cause of this problem may have been that the leader did not have a clear notion of what "on track" actually was and thus did not know when things were drifting. To prevent this from happening, always prepare an agenda for your meetings. Spell out on paper what topics you plan to cover, the sequence of the topics, and the approximate amount of time you plan to spend on each topic. Then use the agenda as a guide to help you keep the meeting on course.

3. **Create a relaxed atmosphere.** The climate or milieu in which a meeting is conducted will have a significant impact on its effectiveness. If the climate is one of rigid formality, you cannot expect a great deal of authentic dialogue. At the other extreme, if the climate is one of "fun and games," the meeting will be equally unproductive. As the leader of the meeting, you can do a great deal to establish an appropriate climate. Through your opening remarks and your manner of communicating throughout, you should endeavor to establish an atmosphere that is conducive to authentic dialogue.

4. **Give everyone a chance to contribute.** Another complaint about meetings is that one or two persons monopolized the meeting. What often happens is that the more extroverted and aggressive individuals will do most of the talking. As a consequence, the less aggressive members will feel left out and that no one was really interested in their ideas. As the leader of the meeting, you must be especially sensitive to the need for getting everyone's involvement. You can do this by calling on the participants individually. In certain situations, such as one in which Jethro monopolizes the discussion, it may be necessary for you to say, "Now we have heard from Jethro. What do the rest of you think?"

5. **Allow and encourage open expression of disagreement.** If the meeting's purpose is one of problem solving or decision making, you can expect disagreement among the various members. Don't make the mistake of suppressing the disagreements. Nor should you try to smooth them over. Rather, let the disagreements be elucidated. Make a special effort to understand each person's views and how these particular views differ from those of others. Then, once the conflicting points of view are out on the table,

move on toward a resolution. Easy to say, of course, but difficult to do. Nevertheless, it is important to appreciate that for authentic dialogue to take place, open expression of disagreement is essential.

6. **Truly listen to the participants.** Throughout the meeting, make a special effort to truly listen to each participant. Ask yourself these questions: What is this person really saying? How does the person feel about what is being said? What is being left unsaid? And postpone evaluation of what is being said until after you are certain that you understand it. Through your questions and paraphrasing of key points, demonstrate to the speaker that you understand both the content and feeling of what has been said. Be a good listener!

7. **Keep the meeting "on track."** A meeting arranged only for information transmission, essentially one-way communication, is fairly easy to keep on track. On the other hand, one that is established for problem solving or decision making, in which group participation is encouraged, may be very difficult to keep on track. What often happens is that a peripheral issue emerges during the discussion, and the group then pursues this peripheral issue. Or, an issue that may be of interest to only one of the participants emerges, and the leader goes down the track of pursuing this particular issue, to the consternation of the other members. Don't let this happen. By continually focusing on the purpose of the meeting and the supporting agenda, keep the meeting on track.

8. **Summarize at the end of the meeting.** At the end of a meeting, the participants want to have a sense of closure — they don't want to be "left hanging." They want to know what has been accomplished during the meeting and what is supposed to happen next. Tell them. In addition to summarizing at certain times during the course of the meeting, provide a "summing up" at the end of the meeting. In crystal-clear terms, spell out to the participants what decisions have been made, what decisions have been left unresolved, what action items have been agreed upon, and who is responsible for what.

9. **Prepare and distribute minutes.** Almost any meeting, except a pure information-transmission meeting, merits a set of minutes: a written record of the agreements arrived at during the meeting. These minutes can help prevent problems and misunderstandings from

arising in the future. It is not necessary that the minutes be lengthy documents. In most cases, one or two pages should suffice, including only the decisions that were made and the action items with the corresponding responsibilities. Then distribute the minutes to all participants within 24 hours after the close of the meeting.

10. **Evaluate the meeting.** For you to continually improve your leadership effectiveness in meetings, it is essential that you get feedback on how well you are doing. You should evaluate each meeting in terms of two criteria: results and process. In terms of results, did you achieve the stated purpose for the meeting? In terms of process, how well did the group work together? You may be able to answer these questions on the basis of your own observations. In addition, you may find it useful to ask the participants at the end of the meeting how they feel about the meeting in terms of both results and process. Assuming that you have created a climate for authentic dialogue, they probably will tell you. You then can use this feedback to improve future meetings.

ORGANIZATIONAL COMMUNICATION

The leader-manager is expected to be effective in organizational communication. This includes all forms of communication insofar as they pertain to the job of the manager. Communication is the means whereby the manager carries out all of the management functions: planning, organizing, staffing and staff development, directing and leading, and evaluating and controlling. Communication is the leader-manager's most vital tool.

A number of barriers are associated with organizational communication, including failure to communicate to the employees the mission and goals of the organization, failure to communicate where the organization is going and how it plans to get there, failure to provide employees with the information they need to carry out their jobs, and failure to provide accurate and timely feedback. These impediments underlie many organizational problems, such as lack of management credibility and lack of trust. The resolution of these impediments could transform a failing enterprise into a successful one.

The key to effective organizational communication is authentic dialogue. This means that living mutual relations are established between and among persons throughout the organization. There is a climate of honest and open communication — upward, downward, and laterally. In the ideal case, we have the true community: an assemblage of persons working together to achieve common goals, with the relationships based on trust. The trust was brought about through authentic dialogue.

The following are guidelines for achieving effective organizational communication.

1. **Let your people know where the organization is headed.** In *Communicating for Productivity*, Roger D'Aprix stresses that employees generally have three communication needs. "They want to know where the organization is heading and how it will get there and — most important — what all that means to them." In other words, they want to know these three things: (1) the destination, (2) the road map for getting to the destination, and (3) their own role in following the road map to arrive at the destination. If you are successful in dealing with these three issues, you will satisfy a large portion of your staff's communication needs.

2. **Let your people know about the major business issues that are influencing the organization.** D'Aprix goes on to stress that employees want to know about the major business issues that are having an impact on the organization. They want management to define and interpret these issues for them, and they want to know what management plans to do to resolve the issues. To respond to this need, a proactive approach will be far more effective than a reactive approach. Rather than being placed in a defensive position of merely reacting to various rumors about specific issues, management should take the initiative in establishing an ongoing program that periodically informs the staff about the principal issues of the day and what is being done to resolve the issues.

3. **Provide accurate and complete information to your people.** As mentioned before, trust is the glue that holds an organization together. Without trust, very little can be accomplished. Providing accurate and complete information to all of your people is a principal way of achieving trust. Here we can see the sharp distinc-

tion between Machiavellian leadership and transforming leadership. The former relies on deception and manipulation, which leads to distrust. The latter relies on honest and open communication, which leads to trust. You should accept the responsibility for providing your people with accurate and complete information, and when you don't know, simply tell them so.

4. **Make certain that each staff member has the information needed to get the job done.** A significant challenge for you as a manager is to help each of your people obtain the information that he or she needs to get the job done. The information should satisfy at least three criteria: accuracy, interpretability, and timeliness. Facilitating this process calls for empathy: You must be able to put yourself in the place of each of your people and help determine the information needs of each. Then, do whatever is reasonably possible to help meet these information needs.

5. **Let your people know what is expected of them.** Employees want to know what is expected of them. They want to know about the job requirements, job standards, and policies and procedures. Tell them. Don't keep them guessing. Through effective face-to-face communication, you should let your people know what is expected. In addition, this oral communication should be supplemented by at least three forms of written communication: a job description, performance objectives (which should be developed *with* the employee), and the organization's policies and procedures.

6. **Manage by walking around.** An indispensable part of organizational communication is managing by walking around. Many communication needs can be satisfied through meetings and written communication, but there will still be a lack. A significant portion of your workweek should be devoted to managing by walking around: interacting with your people on a one-to-one basis to discuss their concerns. This is organizational communication at its best. Nothing can replace it.

7. **Actively seek ideas and opinions from your staff.** When you are managing by walking around, actively seek ideas and opinions from your people. The point to appreciate is that your people are much closer to their jobs than you are. Their views on specific problems and how to correct them undoubtedly will have merit,

so listen to them. And be certain to follow a basic rule expressed by Lee Iacocca: Whenever an employee presents a suggestion to you, be sure to get back to the employee with an answer. Otherwise, the employee won't submit any more suggestions.

8. **Give individual staff members accurate and timely feedback on their performance.** Improvement of job performance depends on knowledge of results. The feedback must be accurate and timely. One of the greatest disservices to employees is to let them go on and on without letting them know how they are doing. On the other hand, one of the greatest services is to provide them with accurate and timely feedback and with concrete suggestions on how they can improve their performance. It is important to bear in mind that negative feedback is better than zero feedback. Whenever a situation calls for your giving negative feedback, do it in a constructive manner and in private.

9. **Keep your people informed about the progress of the unit.** As mentioned previously, employees want to know "Where are we going and how do we plan to get there?" In addition, they want to know "How are we doing?" They want to know about the progress of the work unit. Tell them. An essential part of your job is to set up regularly scheduled meetings to report on the unit's progress. In these meetings, it would be appropriate to review the unit's objectives, which objectives have been achieved, which objectives have not been achieved, and what the problems are. Then solicit ideas from your staff for dealing with the problems. This is teamwork at its best.

10. **"Walk the talk."** *In A Passion for Excellence*, Peters and Austin stress the importance of consistency between actions and words:

> To your team, you (as leader) are your enacted priorities, no more and no less. The mundane, minute-to-minute choices you make as you do your own job are the most powerful teachers. Your people won't miss a beat. So look in the mirror again . . . on and off the field you set the example that others will follow. Do you walk the talk? [p. 337]

* * * * *

In sum, we cannot stress too much the importance of communication. The leader-manager's primary function is to create a vision and then to implement the vision. This cannot be accomplished without communication.

Communication is the means whereby the leader-manager gets the job done. Without communication, a leader-manager would be like a quarterback without a football, a baton twirler without a baton, or a tuba player without a tuba. It would be hard to imagine.

To be an effective communicator, the leader-manager must make a commitment to authentic dialogue. This commitment should be manifested in four different forms of communication: interpersonal communication, written communication, oral presentations, and meetings. These four forms of communication should be used to bring about effective organizational communication.

I close with Roger D'Aprix's challenge to all and each of us:

> Communication is not separate from managing. It is managing. Or, better said, management is communication. This insight is crucial to the task of consistent and well managed communication. Indeed, if we are convinced of that, there is no choice about good organizational communication. If we are to manage our people well, we must communicate well. The two are the same task. (*Communicating for Productivity*, p. 27)

VIII

Empowering

Woodrow Wilson called for leaders who, by boldly inter-
preting the nation's conscience, could lift a people out of
their everyday selves. That people can be lifted *into* their
better selves is the secret of transforming leadership.

James MacGregor Burns
Leadership

---

*The Importance of Motivation • Limitations of the Carrot-and-Stick Ap-
proach • Lifting People into Their Better Selves • The Hierarchy of Human
Needs • Guidelines for Effective Motivation • The Challenge for Every
Manager*

THE IMPORTANCE OF MOTIVATION

In *The Human Side of Enterprise*, Douglas McGregor stresses the
importance of motivation:

> Many managers would agree that the effectiveness of their
> organizations would be at least doubled if they could
> discover how to tap the unrealized potential present in their
> human resources. [p. 4]

What these managers are concerned about is human motivation.
They are seeking ways to better motivate their people. They want
to tap the "unrealized potential."

McGregor's message is echoed by Lee Iacocca:

> I've always felt that a manager has achieved a great deal
> when he's able to motivate one other person. When it comes
> to making the place run, motivation is everything. You
> might be able to do the work of two people, but you can't
> *be* two people. Instead, you have to inspire the next guy
> down the line and get him to inspire *his* people. (*Iacocca*,
> p. 9)

Iacocca is accenting the multiplier effect. Assume that you have
five people reporting to you and that each of these five has five people reporting to him or her. If you inspire your five direct reports
and they then inspire their direct reports, you could have a considerable impact on 25 people. And so it goes throughout the entire
organization.

The importance of motivation is highlighted in this well known
equation:

$$\text{Performance} = f(\text{Ability} \times \text{Motivation} \times \text{Environment})$$

The equation tells us that a given job holder's performance is a
function of three interacting factors: ability (knowledge, skill, experience), motivation (the desire to perform well), and the environment (the physical and social milieu in which the individual works).
To manage for excellence, the manager must give due attention to
all three factors, but we are focusing here on only the second factor
in the equation — motivation.

Because this basic equation has been implanted in my mind for
so many years, a comment by a young supervisor in one of my management seminars took me aback. Jim, who had been a manager
for less than a year, was supervising a group of eight or nine engineers.
After I had introduced the topic of motivation, Jim made this comment: "I never thought that motivation was part of my job. I just
assumed that this was something my people brought with them to
their jobs. They are professionals, you know." I have often reflected
on this comment, and I have wondered how many other managers
of professional staff might share Jim's view.

We know from research and from experience that the manager's
impact on employee motivation is profound. This impact can be
either positive or negative.

Consider an example of two different individual contributors working on two different projects under two different project managers. With regard to ability, Jeremiah and Jennifer have a great deal in common. They both hold degrees in computer science from the same university; they both graduated with a 3.5 point-hour-ratio; they both scored in the same decile on the Graduate Record Examination; and they both have three years of experience in the computer sciences department.

When it comes to actual job performance, however, the similarity between these two computer scientists ends. Jeremiah barely "puts in his time." He is physically present at the job for eight hours each day but does not appear to be psychologically present; his thoughts are elsewhere. He frequently looks at his watch to find out how much longer to quitting time. Jeremiah's marginal performance is now placing his job in jeopardy. Jennifer, on the other hand, is truly present at the job; her thoughts are focused on the job. She always turns out quality work and continually looks for ways to be more innovative and more efficient in her work. It is agreed by everyone involved in the project that Jennifer is a highly productive worker.

As we contrast these two computer scientists, the issue is not one of ability but one of motivation. In comparing their relative contributions to their projects, we might find a difference of at least three to one, even though they are both working roughly eight hours each day.

The question then becomes: What impact do the project managers have on the motivation of these two individuals? Certainly some of the motivation must come from within. But assuming that these two computer scientists are both working for their respective project managers on a full-time basis for a period of six months, how much of their motivation is determined by their project managers? In presenting this question to several hundred managers in management seminars, I have found the responses to range from 10% to 90%. The most frequent response is in the 40–50% range. I believe this estimate would be borne out by the results of empirical research.

In addressing the subject of motivation, a useful starting point is to consider the three fundamental questions posed by Daniel Katz and Robert Kahn in their chapter on "Motivational Patterns and Performance":

1. What are the *types of behavior* required for effective organizational functioning?

2. What different *motivational patterns* are used and can be used to evoke the required behaviors in organizational settings?
3. What are the *conditions for eliciting* a given motivational pattern in an organizational setting?

Consider a new department manager who wants to focus on collaborative efforts between and among the four work units within the department. The department has had a history of internal competition and conflict, which has resulted in many missed business opportunities and less-than-desired financial performance. The new department manager realizes that the key to the department's future success will be collaboration across work units. She first asks: *What types of behavior* (such as working as a team on interunit projects) do we need for collaboration? She next asks: What *motivational patterns* (such as a win-win attitude) can be used to evoke the required behaviors? She then asks: What *should be done* (such as modifying the reward system) to bring about the desired motivational patterns?

With these three interrelated questions in mind, we now ask: How should leader-managers go about the job of motivating their people?

It is useful to consider the question in the light of the distinction between two types of leadership: transactional and transforming. As indicated in Figure 21, these two different types of leadership employ distinctly different approaches to motivation. And the results are distinctly different!

Transactional leadership relies on the carrot-and-stick approach to motivation. The "carrot" is held out by the supervisor in the form of possible rewards: pay increase, promotion, better job assignment, etc. If these potential rewards don't work, then lurking in the background is the "stick" in the form of possible punishments: no pay increase, no promotion, a worse job assignment, etc. This is the pure market economy. We are talking about commodities of exchange for labor. There is nothing really complex about the underlying rationale, and it is accepted by no small number of managers as iron-clad logic. It worked for their own bosses, as well as for their bosses' bosses, so surely it will work for them.

Today, some question the merits of transactional leadership and the carrot-and-stick approach to motivation. They propose an alternative approach. As its principal means of motivation, transforming leadership relies on empowerment. With power being defined as the capability for doing or accomplishing something, "empowerment" means to give power to followers. Leaders empower their people by increasing their capability for doing or accomplishing something.

In the words of Bennis and Nanus, "Power's reciprocal is empowerment." Power and empowerment are two sides of the same coin. When leaders empower their people, a remarkable thing happens: The

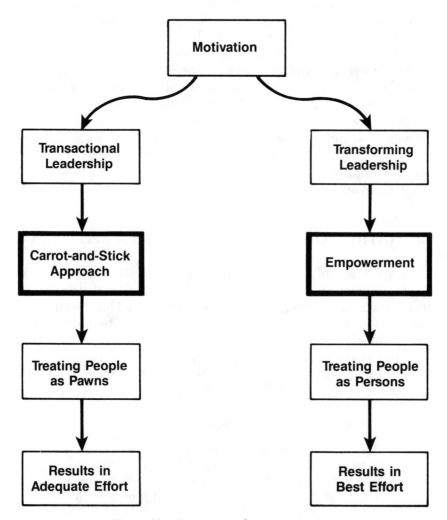

Figure 21. Two approaches to motivation.

leaders themselves *gain in power*. As one side of the coin is enlarged, the other side increases a corresponding amount.

Pragmatic managers then ask the bottom-line question: With regard to these two different approaches to motivation, what is their relative effectiveness? They ask in unison: "What about the results?"

In response to the question, we can offer a general statement. First, though, the statement calls for a qualification. The answer is based on the assumption that you are supervising people who are psychologically mature and you are working in an environment that is conducive to transforming leadership. It does not necessarily apply if you are supervising people found lacking in maturity and/or you are working in an environment that inhibits transforming leadership.

Given this assumption, I can assert with considerable confidence that empowerment will be superior to the carrot-and-stick approach. The principal reason for the superiority of empowerment is found in the way people are treated. Because the carrot-and-stick approach treats people as *pawns*, they will put forth only adequate effort, just enough to attain the rewards or to avoid the punishment. But inasmuch as empowerment treats people as *persons*, they will put forth their best effort—go beyond what is expected of them. And this is what motivation is all about.

LIMITATIONS OF THE CARROT-AND-STICK APPROACH

A great deal of evidence suggests that motivation is found lacking in large numbers of American workers and that their work effort has worsened during the last several decades. This situation has prompted many people to ask: "What has happened to the American work ethic?"

The present situation is placed in perspective through a Public Agenda Foundation report authored by Daniel Yankelovich and John Immerwahr. Their findings should give all managers reason for concern.

According to Yankelovich and Immerwahr:

> The Public Agenda research found that most people say that they are giving considerably less to their jobs than they believe they could give and, in principle, are willing to give. A majority feel that under the right conditions they would significantly increase their performance. (p. 407 in Williamson)

The Public Agenda Foundation report highlights these findings:

- Only about one out of four workers indicate that they are performing to their full capacity and are being as productive as they are capable of being. Most people indicate that they could increase their productivity significantly.
- About half of the work force state that they do not put a great deal of effort into their jobs over and above what is required.
- The majority of jobholders believe that other people are not working as hard as they used to. (This may not be true, but it is their perception.)

The authors of the report contend that the American workplace is currently structured in ways that undermine the strong work ethic values that people bring to their jobs. These are some of the problems:

- **A mismatch between people's values and the existing reward system:** About half of the work force feel that there is a mismatch between their own values and the rewards and incentives associated with their jobs.
- **Disincentives:** Almost half of the work force perceive no relationship between pay and performance.
- **Managers who don't motivate:** About three-fourths of the work force believe that managers in general do not know how to motivate workers.

Yankelovich and Immerwahr conclude their report with this observation:

> In sum, we conclude that the American economy is failing to utilize one of its most powerful resources — a widespread commitment to the work ethic. Although many people want to work hard and do good work for its own sake, the workplace is structured in ways that discourage rather than support the norm. As a result, people work below their potential and do less than they want to. The demands of jobholders for managers who know how to motivate . . . reflect people's desire to give more to their jobs than they are currently giving. [p. 416]

The indictment that American managers do not know how to motivate workers is cause for concern. A number of astute observers of organizational behavior would contend that the chief problem lies in reliance on the carrot-and-stick approach to motivation. One of

these observers, Harry Levinson, reports on one of his surveys in the
paper, "Asinine Attitudes Toward Motivation":

> Frequently, I have asked executives this question: What is
> the dominant philosophy of motivation in American
> management? Almost invariably, they quickly agree that
> it is the carrot-and-stick philosophy, reward and punish-
> ment. Then I ask them to close their eyes for a moment,
> and to form a picture in their mind's eye with a carrot at
> one end and a stick at the other. When they have done so,
> I then ask them to describe the central image in that pic-
> ture. Most frequently they respond that the central figure
> is a jackass.

The problem with the carrot-and-stick approach is that it treats
people as pawns rather than persons. How would you feel if you were
being treated as a pawn — as an object to be manipulated to further
another person's ends? You undoubtedly would feel angry. You might
even rebel. At best, you would give no more than a moderate amount
of effort to your work. You certainly would not give your best effort.

It appears that many American workers are operating on only
three or four cylinders rather than seven or eight. And I do not believe
that anyone is calling for employees to work much more than the
normal eight-hour day. This is not the problem. What is being called
for is that American workers — during the normal eight-hour day
operate on seven or eight cylinders.

Perhaps the most significant finding in the Public Agenda survey
is that many American workers are saying that *they would significantly increase their performance under the right conditions*; that
is, that they would be willing to operate on seven or eight cylinders.
The question then becomes: What are the *right* conditions?

The answer lies in a move from the carrot-and-stick approach
to that of empowerment, from transactional leadership to transforming leadership.

LIFTING PEOPLE INTO THEIR BETTER SELVES

James MacGregor Burns has proposed that the secret of transforming leadership is lifting people into their better selves. To some, this
notion may have a mystical or transcendental ring to it. It is not the
language of results-oriented pragmatists, but it may be one of the

most practical notions generated during the past decade. It may be the key to transforming nonproductive workers into productive ones. Thus, it will be worthwhile to consider what is meant by "lifting people into their better selves." First, though, we will look at what is meant by the "self."

The self is an elusive concept, defying any clear and concise description. Yet each person is indeed aware of the existence of his or her own self. Within the healthy personality is a central core that does seem unchangeable, remaining rather constant throughout one's life. It is the "I" that looks out at the world, rather than the "me" that is being looked at. Perhaps no one else really knows this "I," but you and I certainly know our own "I's." We are absolutely certain of its existence, so much so that there is no reason to even question its existence. Nevertheless, if asked to describe this entity or phenomenon which we call the self, we find it most difficult to offer any precise description.

The self may be viewed as the active center of one's life. In the healthy personality, the various facets of the person's life are united around this active center. The results of clinical research suggest that there is a direct correlation between the degree to which the different elements of one's life are united around the active center and the degree of mental health.

Some years ago, a well-known actress left Hollywood and her career in search of her "real self." She explained her departure by saying that she had taken her roles too seriously. During the production of each film in which she starred, she essentially "became" the person whom she was portraying. The positive result of this professional commitment was the achievement of acclaim and numerous awards, but the negative consequence was that she awakened one day to the realization that she did not know who she was. She could not distinguish between her "real self" and the various personages that she had played so well. Thus, she abandoned a succeccful career to embark on a search for her self.

The question then becomes: How many selves does a given individual have? Does a person have only one self, or may he or she have more than one self? A framework for answering the question is provided by Hazel Markus and Paula Nurius in their paper, "Possible Selves." These two authors suggest that each individual has a repertoire of possible selves:

> Possible selves represent individuals' ideas of what they might become, what they would like to become, and what they are afraid of becoming. An individual's repertoire of possible selves can be viewed as the cognitive manifestation of enduring goals, aspirations, motives, fears, and threats. Possible selves provide the specific self-relevant form, meaning, organization, and direction to these dynamics. As such, *they provide the essential link between the self-concept and motivation.*

Each person carries in his or her consciousness three different representations of the self: the past self, the now self, and the possible future self. Your past self is your view of what you were in the past; your now self is what you are at this moment; and your possible future self is the self that you might become.

Further, most people carry in their consciousnesses two versions of the possible future self: the *desired* possible future self and the *undesired* possible future self. The desired is the self that you very much would like to become, and the undesired is the self that you definitely do not want to become.

Building on the seminal paper by Markus and Nurius, I have constructed the framework shown in Figure 22. At the center of the diagram is the now self, that which you are at this moment in time. At the two poles are the ideal self (the person that you would like to become) and the feared self (the person that you do not want to become). Intermediate between your now self and your ideal self is your higher self, which is the "better self" that you have actually been at certain times. And intermediate between your now self and your feared self is your lower self, which is the "worse self" that you have actually been at certain times. Thus, between the two poles of the ideal self and the feared self, most people fluctuate between their higher selves and their lower selves. (Only saints are able to move continually upward.)

Vacillation between one's higher self and one's lower self is well illustrated in the legend of Faust. As some readers will recall, Faust signs with the devil a pact that commits his soul to hell in return for 24 hours of unlimited pleasure and power. This was the basic agreement: Mephistopheles (the devil) will be Faust's servant during life and will provide anything he wants if Faust will agree to become his servant after death — that is, to sell his soul.

The side wager is between the Lord and Mephistopheles. The

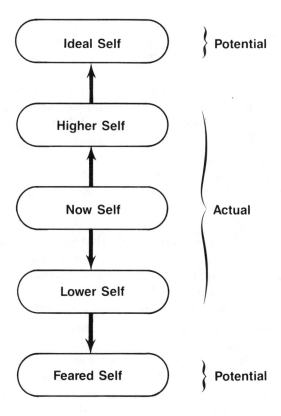

Figure 22.   Possible selves.

Lord, the paragon of perfection toward which people strive, believes that Faust will rise to his "higher self." Mephistopheles, the spirit of negativism and nihilism, is convinced that Faust will shrink to his "lower self." The continual movement between these two selves is the story line of the entire legend.

The conflict between the two selves is expressed by Faust with great emotion:

> Two souls, alas, are housed within my breast,
> And each will wrestle for the mastery there.
> The one has passion's craving crude for love,
> And hugs a world where sweet the senses rage;
> The other longs for pastures fair above,
> Leaving the murk for lofty heritage.
> (Goethe's *Faust*, p. 67)

How does the story turn out? In Christopher Marlowe's version of the legend, *Tragical History of Doctor Faustus* (1588), Mephistopheles wins the wager. But in Goethe's version, *Faust* (1808 and 1832), the Lord wins. I personally prefer Goethe's version. But that is beside the point. The point is that this reflective story reveals the constant struggle between one's higher and one's lower selves. It deals with the individual's sense of alienation and the need to come to grips with the world in which one lives. The story is as applicable today as it was in medieval times.

Many are those who can identify with Faust in his quandary. Each person has an ideal self that beckons. But pulling in the opposite direction is the feared self that seduces. Between these two poles are the higher self and the lower self that reflect the continual vacillation of many people's lives. Oh, that they could truly become their higher selves on an enduring basis and shed their lower selves, but this may be too much of a load for the individual to take on alone. A helping hand is needed.

The helping hand can be provided by the leader. By taking a personal interest in the development of each of his or her people, the effective leader-manager is able to identify each person's ideal self and then help the person move toward it. Potentiality is transformed into actuality. This is the essence of what is meant by "a helping relationship." As a consequence of the reciprocal relationship between leader and follower, the leader also is stimulated and elevated. This is what transforming leadership is all about.

THE HIERARCHY OF HUMAN NEEDS*

The notion of "lifting people into their better selves" can be elucidated by viewing it in the light of Abraham Maslow's hierarchy of human needs. Since most readers will be familiar with the basic concepts of Maslow's theory of motivation, it will not be necessary to discuss them in any great detail. But just to make certain that we are all working from the same conceptual framework, it will be worthwhile to simply summarize some of the key features of Maslow's theory.

Before Maslow's pioneering work in the area of motivation, most psychologists took a purely behavioral approach to studying motiva-

---

*This section is reproduced from *Management in Action* by William D. Hitt; Battelle Press, 1985.

tion. Essentially, this was a stimulus-response approach in which the investigators would carry out a three-step process: (1) define and measure behavioral aspects of motivation; (2) define and measure environmental stimuli that might affect motivation; and (3) correlate the environmental stimuli and the behavioral aspects. Although considered to be a rigorous approach to the study of motivation, the behavioral approach bore little fruit.

In sharp contrast to the behavioral approach, Maslow stressed that motivation lies *within* the human organism and can be understood only by viewing it from within. In his book, *Toward a Psychology of Being*, Maslow presents his basic view of motivation:

> Many of the problems that have plagued writers as they attempted to define and delimit motivation are a consequence of the exclusive demand for behavioral, externally observable criteria. The original criterion of motivation and the one that is still used by all human beings except behavioral psychologists is the subjective one. *I am motivated when I feel desire or want or yearning or wish or lack.* [p. 22]

Maslow defined motivation in terms of *needs*. A need signifies a discrepancy between what the individual *has* and what he or she *desires*. The individual is "driven" or "motivated" to reduce or eliminate the discrepancy. Thus, if there is no discrepancy between what exists and what is desired, there is no motivation.

Maslow postulated that there are basic needs common to all of humankind. These are inborn and are found in all members of the human species, regardless of race or culture. The basic needs are grouped into these five categories:

1. **Physiological needs:** need for oxygen, water, food, rest, etc.
2. **Safety needs:** need for security, stability, dependency, protection, structure, order, law, limits, strength in the protector.
3. **Belongingness needs:** need for affectionate relations with other people, need for a place in one's group or family.
4. **Self-esteem needs:** need for self-respect and for the esteem of others.
5. **Self-actualization:** desire for self-fulfillment, to become all that one is capable of becoming.

According to Maslow, these basic needs are related to each other in a hierarchical order. When one need is satisfied, this does not bring about a state of rest but, rather, it brings into consciousness another "higher" need. Wanting and desiring still continue but at a higher level. As indicated in Figure 23, the hierarchical order of needs progresses from physiological needs, to safety needs, to belongingness needs, to self-esteem needs, and finally to self-actualization.

Maslow throws light on the hierarchy by noting that one's higher nature rests upon one's lower nature, needing it as a foundation and collapsing without it. He suggests that, for the majority of humankind, the higher nature is inconceivable without a satisfied lower nature; perhaps the only way to develop this higher nature is to fulfill and gratify the lower nature first. One's higher nature clearly rests on the existence of a fairly good environment, both present and past.

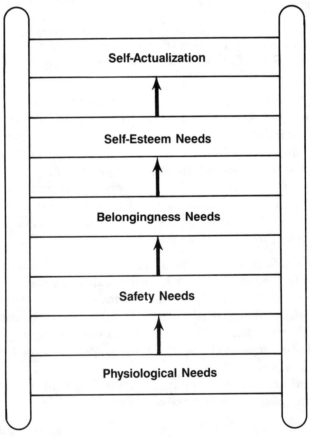

Figure 23.   The hierarchy of human needs.

From his many years of research in the area of human motivation, Maslow found that even though only a very small percentage of the population ever reaches the top rung of the needs hierarchy (that is, achieves self-actualization), the psychologically healthy individual continually advances in the hierarchy. Conversely, the psychologically unhealthy individual is very likely to remain at a lower tier in the hierarchy.

Maslow found that a person's position in the hierarchy is related to a number of other factors. He found, for example, that when individuals *are not* moving toward self-actualization, they are likely to be characterized by boredom, tension, neurotic anxiety, low frustration tolerance, cynicism and despair, psychosomatic illness, low job satisfaction, and low productivity. On the positive side, when individuals *are* moving toward self-actualization, they are likely to be more open and spontaneous, more tolerant of frustration, more courageous, kinder toward others, more creative, more satisfied with their jobs, and more productive.

Based on Maslow's findings, the message to managers seems clear. Managers should endeavor to understand the needs of their people as individual persons and then create an environment that will help them move up the hierarchy. Inasmuch as motivation lies within the individual, the manager cannot motivate directly; nevertheless, there is a great deal that can be done by the manager that will have an impact on the individual jobholder's motivation. As a result, the individual employee will be more highly motivated and will be more productive. If this happens for most employees within a particular work unit, then the unit itself will be more productive. So it goes for the entire organization.

In sum, the principal point here is that Maslow's theory of motivation provides us with a framework for answering the question: What should be done to lift people into their better selves? There is a straightforward answer: Do whatever is reasonably possible to help your people move up the needs hierarchy. *Empower your people by helping them move toward self-actualization.*

In the words of James MacGregor Burns:

> The nature of leadership skills will vary with the situation, but one talent all leaders must possess — the capacity to perceive needs of followers in relationship to their own, to help followers move toward fuller self-realization and self-actualization along with the leaders themselves. (*Leadership*, p. 116)

GUIDELINES FOR EFFECTIVE MOTIVATION

We now shift from theory to practice. The theory is guided by the thesis that transforming leaders lift people into their better selves by helping them move up the hierarchy of human needs. The practical question then becomes: What should managers do to bring that about? Specifically, what should managers do on a day-to-day basis to help their people move up the hierarchy of human needs?

Following are 25 guidelines for action. We start with the physiological needs and move upward in the hierarchy to self-actualization. Some of the guidelines obviously call for the approval of upper management, but the majority of them could be applied by every manager within the organization, regardless of level.

Physiological Needs

> The physiological needs are the most prepotent of all the needs. For an individual who is missing everything in life in an extreme fashion, it is most likely that the major motivation for this person would be the physiological needs rather than any of the others. [pp. 36–37]
>
> Abraham Maslow

1. **Provide good physical surroundings.** The physical surroundings need not be elegant, but they should be sufficient to meet the requirements for a productive work environment. Attention should be given to lighting, temperature, noise control, smoke control, and physical spacing. Do whatever is reasonably possible to create a physical environment that furthers productive work rather than constrains it.
2. **Eliminate safety hazards.** Assume responsibility for the safety of your people. Be ever vigilant in identifying potential safety hazards, be they in the production line or in the office. Be sensitive to both physical safety hazards and environmental safety hazards. And bear in mind the admonition passed on to us by our grandparents: An ounce of prevention is worth a pound of cure.
3. **Prevent excessive stress.** It is important to appreciate that there is a curvilinear relation between the amount of stress in the workplace and job performance. A moderate amount

of stress can increase performance, but high levels of stress usually will cause a decline in performance. Thus, the guideline is to create an environment that averts *excessive* stress. To this end, avoid crisis management.

4. **Make certain that all of your people are able to take their vacations.** Some jobholders get themselves in positions of being so indispensable that they are not able to take their vacations. Thus, when a new year starts, they may lose some or all of their accrued vacation. Do not allow this to happen — because eventually you may be managing people who are suffering from burnout. And make certain that your people take off for more than one or two days at a time.

5. **Promote good health.** In general, employees who are in good physical health are more alert, are less prone to illness, and are more productive than employees who are in poor physical health. Do whatever you can to promote good physical health among your people. If health programs do not exist, push for exercise facilities, intramural sports, and a health office that provides annual physical examinations.

Safety Needs

> If the physiological needs are fairly well gratified, then there emerges a new set of needs: the safety and security needs. Essentially everything that may be said about the physiological needs is equally true — but to a less degree — about these needs. The human being may equally well be wholly dominated by them. [p. 39]
>
> Abraham Maslow

1. **Achieve a match between job demands and staff capabilities.** When people are in jobs in which the demands *are greater than* their capabilities, they suffer from worry and anxiety. When they are in jobs in which the demands are *substantially below* their capabilities, they suffer from boredom first and then anxiety. Do whatever you can to get your people in the "flow channel," where there is a match between job demands and staff capabilities (allowing, of course, for "stretch" assignments).

2. **Let your people know what is expected of them.** Your peo-

ple have a need and a right to know exactly what is expected
of them in terms of job requirements, work standards, work
quality, etc. Further, they should understand the criteria on
which they will be judged. Tell them. They should not be
expected to figure this out on their own.

3. **Provide candid and timely feedback on performance.** One
of your most important responsibilities is to give your people honest feedback on their performance. Because feedback
affects both learning and motivation, it is essential to productivity. When giving feedback, be specific, timely, and
constructive. And remember: negative feedback is better than
no feedback.

4. **Establish a rational compensation program.** A compensation
program should be based on a well thought out philosophy
and administered in a manner that is consistent with the
philosophy. Do whatever you can to assure a clear relation
between pay and performance. To the extent that you can
link pay to actual job performance, you will diminish the
importance of internal politics as a means of "getting ahead."

5. **Provide job security based on performance.** With a sample
of several thousand workers, we would expect to find a curvilinear relation between job security and job performance.
This means that there is a positive relation between job security and job performance *up to a point*, but beyond this
point, performance is likely to decline. The message for managers is that you should not attempt to maximize job security;
rather, you should endeavor to *optimize* it. To this end, tie
job security to job performance.

Belongingness Needs

> If both the physiological and safety needs are fairly
> well gratified, there will emerge the love and af-
> fection and belongingness needs. The whole cy-
> cle will repeat itself with this new focus. Now the
> person will hunger for affectionate relations with
> people in general, for a place in his or her group
> or family. The individual will strive with great in-
> tensity to achieve this goal. [p. 43]
>
> Abraham Maslow

1. **Involve your people in goal setting and planning.** To help your people feel that they are vital members of the team, involve them in developing goals and plans for the work unit. Involve them in addressing these two questions: Where are we going? and How do we plan to get there? The end result should be a team of people who are asserting, "These are *our* goals; this is *our* plan."

2. **Involve your people in team problem solving.** Whenever a consequential problem that affects the entire group arises, consider involving your people in solving the problem. In a team meeting, you should lay out the problem-solving process and then guide your people through it. The chances are reasonably good that the solution arrived at will be better than that which you would have generated alone. If your people are the ones who must implement the solution, then the chances are exceedingly good that they will be more highly motivated to do so than if you had solved the problem on a solo basis and then instructed them to implement the solution.

3. **Involve your people in team decision making.** Just as with problem solving, when an important decision that affects the entire group arises, consider involving your people in the decision. Bear in mind Norman Maier's basic equation: $ED = Q \times A$. The *effective decision* (one that is successfully executed) is a function of the *quality* of the decision times the *acceptance* by those who must implement it.

4. **Involve your people in reviewing the unit's performance.** As a manager, it is easy for you to slide into a groove of reviewing the unit's performance on a solo basis. You should consider involving your people in this function. When the time arrives for generating ideas for corrective action, your people are likely to make significant contributions. And when the time arrives to implement the corrective actions, then certainly they will be more highly motivated to do so if they have been involved in actually deciding on the steps needed for corrective action.

5. **Involve your people in team development activities.** At least once each year you should take your people (that is, your direct reports) off site for a team building activity. Here you will find that an effective strategy is to use a discrepancy

model: (1) What kind of team would we like to be? (2) What kind of team are we today? (3) What are the discrepancies between what we are and what we would like to be? and (4) What specific actions should be taken to reduce the discrepancies? After the meeting, implement the recommendations and follow up.

Self-Esteem Needs

> All people in our society (with a few pathological exceptions) have a need for a stable, high evaluation of themselves, for self-respect, and for the esteem of others. Satisfaction of the self-esteem need leads to feelings of self-confidence, worth, strength, capability, and adequacy, of being useful and necessary in the world. [p. 45]
>
> Abraham Maslow

1. **Treat each person with dignity and respect.** Treating each of your people with dignity and respect should be such an easy thing to do. Through your words and actions, convey to each of your people that you view him or her as a unique human being, as a person of worth. In the words of Immanuel Kant, "Treat your people as ends in themselves, never merely as means to some higher end."

2. **Show each person how his or her work contributes to worthwhile ends.** Experience shows that jobholders can be motivated in carrying out very mundane tasks if they understand how these tasks contribute to worthwhile ends. They are "turned on" by the ends, and they realize that the mundane work must be done to achieve these ends. Make certain that you give sufficient attention to explaining to your people how their day-to-day activities contribute to higher ends.

3. **Promote self-management on the part of each of your people.** Self-esteem is linked closely to a feeling of freedom and control over one's own work. To the extent that jobholders feel that they can control and direct their own day-to-day activities, they will have more self-esteem. A practical way to bring about this state of affairs is through management by objectives. Assuming that you and the staff member reach agreement on the staff member's performance objectives for

the coming year, then the latter should be able to direct his or her efforts toward these objectives with only minimal supervision.

4. **Ask your people for their ideas and opinions.** What a great boost to self-esteem: "My boss asked me for my ideas on what should be done. That made my day." Do it with sincerity. And be sure to give your people credit for their ideas and contributions.

5. **Recognize individuals for good work.** Some managers can be characterized as "bad finders." It is as though they carry in their heads a template that represents the ideal, and they then zap any individual who deviates from this ideal. This is an excellent way to *demotivate* people. Certainly you cannot afford to ignore errors and examples of poor performance, but place them in perspective by evaluating them in the light of the individual's total performance. As you consider this total performance, make a special point of giving recognition for good work.

Self-Actualization Needs

> Even if all these needs are satisfied (physiological, safety, belongingness, self-esteem), we may still often (if not always) expect that a new discontent and restlessness will soon develop unless individuals are doing what *they*, individually, are fitted for. Musicians must make music, artists must paint, poets must write if they are to be ultimately at peace with themselves. What individuals *can be*, *they must* be. They must be true to their own nature. [p. 46]
>
> Abraham Maslow

1. **Show a personal interest in the development of each of your people.** One of the most important things that you can do as a manager is to take the time to build a personal relationship with each of your people. Get to know them as individuals. Show them that you are genuinely interested in their development. This involvement obviously will demand a substantial amount of your time, but the return will be in the form of a more highly motivated work unit.

2. **Identify the personal goals of each of your people.** As you develop a personal relationship with your people, find out about their personal goals. What do they want to do? What do they want to accomplish? What do they want to become? What do they want to be recognized for? Answers to questions such as these will help you form a mental picture of each person's ideal self.

3. **Provide effective on-the-job training and coaching.** By having a clear understanding of each person's long-range goals, you will be in an advantageous position to provide counseling and coaching that will help the person move toward these goals. You can do this through coaching. Be a *good coach.* Ask good questions; be a good listener; be supportive; make practical suggestions; be candid.

4. **Provide opportunities for formal education and training.** Your understanding of each person's long-range goals also will place you in a favorable position to recommend formal education and training courses. Most organizations have limited budgets for the support of such programs, hence the need to be selective. You should endeavor to identify specific courses that would contribute to each person's goal-achievement and then do whatever is needed to obtain the approvals and financial support for participation in these courses.

5. **Provide career planning assistance.** The basic unit of good career planning is the ongoing dialogue between the jobholder and the supervisor. Although it is acknowledged that the primary responsibility for career planning should rest with the jobholder, you can be of considerable assistance in this endeavor. Demonstrate to each of your people that you are genuinely interested in his or her career development. Find out about the career aspirations of each of your people; find out about the career opportunities within the organization; then assist each of your people in achieving a match between the two. This is what career planning is all about.

This total set of guidelines is a "large order." We have covered the gamut from physiological needs to self-actualization. Implementing the guidelines will be no easy task. Obstacles will be encountered along the way, but if you are able to overcome them, you are sure to be rewarded in the form of more highly motivated people and a more productive work unit. What is more, you will be rewarded by the personal satisfaction that comes from being a transforming leader — a leader-manager who is able to lift people into their better selves.

THE CHALLENGE FOR EVERY MANAGER

As we draw to the end of this chapter on motivation, it is time for a recapitulation of the argument. We can do this through the logic provided by our implicit outline: prologue, problem, proposition, principles, proposal, and prospects.

- The *prologue* identifies two principal methods of motivation: the carrot-and-stick approach and empowerment.
- The *problem* with the carrot-and-stick approach is that it treats people as pawns rather than persons.
- The underlying *proposition* is that empowerment is more powerful than the carrot-and-stick approach because it lifts people into their better selves.
- The *principles* associated with lifting people into their better selves are revealed in Maslow's hierarchy of human needs.
- The *proposal* calls for the application of guidelines for action organized within the framework of the needs hierarchy.
- The *prospects* are that the application of the guidelines for action can spell the difference between mediocrity and excellence.

Underlying the entire argument is the sharp difference between transactional leadership and transforming leadership. Transactional leaders rely on a carrot-and-stick approach to motivation and are able to elicit only an "adequate" effort from their employees. In sharp contrast, transforming leaders use empowerment as their principal means of motivation and are able to bring out the best efforts from their people. Getting people "to do their best" is what motivation is all about.

A salient difference between transactional leaders and transforming leaders is found in how they perceive their people. Transactional leaders tend to perceive their people as pawns, as objects to be manipulated to further another person's ends, whereas transforming leaders view people as ends in themselves. Further, transactional leaders tend to perceive people only in terms of their actuality, what they are at this point in time, whereas transforming leaders perceive people in terms of both their actuality *and* their potentiality.

Which is the better of the two approaches? The answer lies in the Golden Rule. Regardless of your particular faith or philosophical orientation, Figure 24 points up the universality of the Golden Rule. If you believe that you should treat others as you would like to be treated, then surely you will choose to be a transforming leader.

If you desire to become an effective transforming leader, then focus on motivation. Get to know each of your people as persons — as unique human beings with unique needs. Learn about their goals and aspirations, their needs for self-actualization. Then do whatever is reasonably possible to help each of your people move toward self-actualization. Help them become their better selves.

You should not delay in confronting the challenge facing you. There is no definitive theory of human motivation, and perhaps there never will be, at least in our lifetimes. But we do have a conceptual framework and associated guidelines for action. For the benefit of your people, your organization, and yourself, you can apply these guidelines *now*.

As you consider how you might apply the guidlines for action, reflect on these words of wisdom by James MacGregor Burns:

> To move from manipulation to power-wielding is to move from checkers to chess. But democratic leadership moves far beyond chess because, as we play the game, the chessmen come alive, the bishops and knights and pawns take part on their own terms and with their own motivations, values, and goals, and the game moves ahead with new momentum, direction, and possibilities. In real life the most practical advice for leaders is not to treat pawns like pawns, nor princes like princes, but all persons like *persons*. (*Leadership*, pp. 461–62)

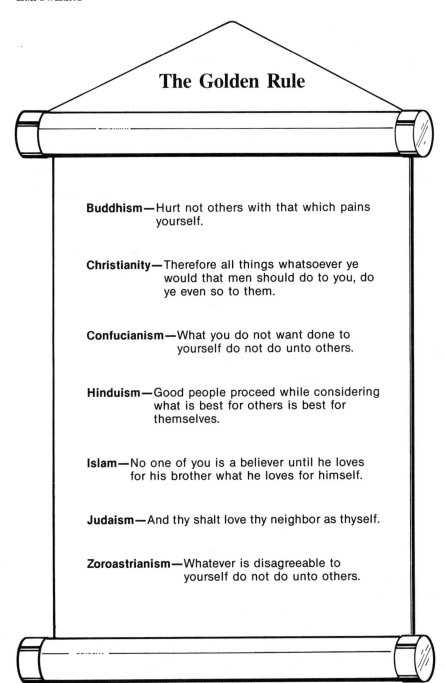

The Golden Rule

Buddhism—Hurt not others with that which pains yourself.

Christianity—Therefore all things whatsoever ye would that men should do to you, do ye even so to them.

Confucianism—What you do not want done to yourself do not do unto others.

Hinduism—Good people proceed while considering what is best for others is best for themselves.

Islam—No one of you is a believer until he loves for his brother what he loves for himself.

Judaism—And thy shalt love thy neighbor as thyself.

Zoroastrianism—Whatever is disagreeable to yourself do not do unto others.

Figure 24.   The Golden Rule.

IX

Coaching

The ideal teacher guides his students but does not pull them along; he urges them to go forward and does not suppress them; he opens the way, but does not take them to the place.

Confucius
"On Education" (Lin Yutang)

The Need for Developmental Managers • Obstacles to Being a Developmental Manager • Success Through the Accomplishment of Others • Attributes of the Developmental Manager • To Become a Developmental Manager • Benefits of Being a Developmental Manager

---

THE NEED FOR DEVELOPMENTAL MANAGERS

In a given time period, large numbers of people face new job responsibilities. This includes both employees just joining the organization and those who are given new job assignments. In the former case, it might be a new secretary faced with learning how to use the word processor, an accountant faced with learning the inner workings of the organization's finance and accounting system, or a computer specialist faced with learning how the management information system operates. In the latter case, we might find an engineer who has just been made a project manager, a production worker who has just been promoted to supervisor, or a supervisor who has just been given a lateral transfer. In all of these cases, the job incumbents are faced with the need to acquire new job skills.

How are these individuals to acquire the new skills needed to carry out their jobs effectively? Basically, there are three alternatives: learning on their own, participating in formal training programs, or receiving on-the-job coaching. There are advantages and disadvantages associated with each.

Learning on one's own is sometimes viewed as a sink-or-swim approach. If the person can make it, "fine," but if not, "too bad." Certainly, this is an approach that fosters initiative, individual responsibility, and self-management. On the other hand, it often proves to be inefficient. Because of lack of direction and assistance, the jobholder may spend large amounts of time in making "false passes" and then correcting the errors. Further, if the self-taught individual learns to carry out specific procedures in an improper manner, it may be very difficult to alter these behaviors later. In fact, it may be worse than "starting from scratch." Thus, most would agree that self-managed learning may be one approach to acquiring new skills, but it should not be the only approach.

Formal training is defined as any instruction that is organized and packaged in a systematic manner to teach specific job skills, and usually in a classroom setting. Today we can identify the salient features of an effective formal training program: it has clearly stated objectives, is job related, actively involves the participants in the learning process, and is systematically evaluated and revised. A training program that satisfies these criteria is likely to show a return on investment. But the major limitation of formal training, even top-notch training, is its restricted accessibility. It has been reported that the average professional employee in the United States will participate in only about three days of formal training each year. Hence, there is simply not enough training to meet the dynamic learning needs of all employees on a continuing basis.

The third approach to acquiring new job skills is through on-the-job training, which is called "coaching." Here we define coaching as on-the-job counseling by the immediate supervisor. While there may be only three days available for formal training, there may be more than 200 days for coaching, anytime the job incumbent and supervisor are together. The major problem associated with coaching is the demand on the supervisor's time. But the effective leader-manager will not use this as an excuse and will simply *make the time* that is needed to provide coaching for each staff member.

The nature of coaching is elucidated by Peters and Austin:

> To coach is largely to facilitate, which literally means "to make easy"— not less demanding, less interesting, or less intense, but less discouraging, less bound up with excessive controls and complications. Coaching is the process of enabling others to act, of building on their strengths. Coaching at its heart involves caring enough about people to take the time to build a personal relationship with them. Easy to say, tough to do. [p. 326]

Consider a manager who does not take this message to heart. Manager A may very well be an intelligent, hard-driving individual but simply does not view coaching as a significant part of the job. Here is a typical response: "I hear what you are saying about job coaching. That's fine in theory, but in the real world I simply don't have time to coach my people. If I am up to my neck in alligators, how do you expect me to find time to coach?"

Then consider a manager who does take the message to heart. Manager B takes a personal interest in the development of each of his or her people. Here is a typical response: "Yes, I do view coaching as one of my most important job functions. Certainly, it takes time, but primarily on the front end of a new job assignment. If I do it right, then I actually *save time* in the long run, because it leads to more self-management on the part of each of my people."

Now consider two employees, one assigned to Manager A and the other assigned to Manager B.

The person reporting to Manager A is suffering from a serious handicap. What is found lacking is the day-to-day feedback, counseling, and encouragement that are needed for effective learning, as well as for effective motivation. While reliance on self-learning undoubtedly will produce some beneficial results, the total learning will be far less than it could be.

The person reporting to Manager B is fortunate indeed. This individual is blessed with a personal relationship with his or her manager, a manager who demonstrates through both words and actions a genuine interest in the development of each employee. And through day-to-day discussions with the manager, the employee continues to learn and to grow.

Then trace the progress of these two employees over a period of, say, two years. With the person reporting to Manager A, we might expect to find about a 20–30% advancement in job growth, which

includes knowledge, skills, and attitudes. But with the person reporting to Manager B, we might expect to find anywhere from 50–100%
advancement in job growth. This difference is sufficiently large to
spell the difference between mediocrity and excellence.

Effective leader-managers view coaching of their staff as one of
their most important job functions. Granted that the managerial
functions of planning, organizing, staffing, directing and leading,
and controlling are important. But right alongside these functions
in importance is that of staff development, and specifically in the
form of on-the-job coaching.

Effective leader-managers have a developmental orientation.
They take a personal interest in the development of each of their
people. They accept and thrive on the challenge of helping to convert potentiality into actuality.

OBSTACLES TO BEING A DEVELOPMENTAL MANAGER

In response to the message regarding the importance of coaching,
there are many managers who will say, "Of course." Others will be
overwhelmed by the obstacles. Indeed, there are some serious
obstacles to being a developmental manager. It is important to consider each.

A commitment to the Lone Ranger model. Many managers attempt to emulate the Lone Ranger. They ride in on their white horses,
defeat the adversary, and ride off into the darkness of the night. The
people all exclaim: "He did it alone!" But it was not quite alone,
because the Lone Ranger did have his trusted assistant, Tonto, at
his side. Fortunately for the Lone Ranger, Tonto has an excellent
grasp of his job responsibilities and the line of authority. He needs
no coaching.

Not viewing coaching as part of the job. In reviewing a large
number of managerial job descriptions, I have found that many of
them have a serious omission: no mention of staff development. It
is as though coaching of staff is not even considered part of the job.
I once mentioned this deficiency to a personnel manager who was
responsible for developing job descriptions, and the reply was quite
disturbing. His response was that job descriptions should focus on
accomplishment of results, and coaching was not a result. Indeed,

transforming human potentiality into actuality is not considered a result. What a pity.

Focusing only on short-term results. Large numbers of managers are "under the gun" to produce short-term results. In years past, managers were expected to produce results on a one-year basis. Of late, however, it seems that the time period has been shortened to three months, and, in some cases, to even one month. Managers working in such an environment find it difficult, and perhaps impossible, to devote adequate attention to the coaching of their staff. Time devoted to coaching is an investment in the future. Spending substantial amounts of time in coaching may not pay off immediately, but if done properly, it is certain to reap benefits in the months and years ahead.

Working in a crisis management environment. Focusing on short-term results often creates a crisis management environment. Such an environment is a serious impediment to effective coaching. Whenever managers are working in a crisis mode and it is necessary to select a staff member for a particular assignment, whom do they typically select? It is someone who has carried out this particular task successfully at least a dozen times previously. In a less stressful environment, it would have been very reasonable to select a person for whom this task would have been a stretch assignment. With appropriate coaching, the individual could have carried out the assignment successfully and then would have been prepared to carry out similar assignments in the future.

Inability or unwillingness to delegate. Many managers are either unable or unwilling to delegate to their staff. We hear them exclaim: "But I can do it better myself." . . . "It would take me too long to explain it." . . . "I don't think Jesse is ready for this assignment." . . . "Mary Beth might make a mistake." . . . "I don't know if I can trust Billy Joe to take on this task." . . . "You know that my neck is out on this one, and they will hold me accountable." This, of course, is only a partial listing of reasons given for not delegating. The entire list might take several pages. This deficiency may be the chief barrier that prevents many otherwise good managers from moving up the management ladder.

Lack of skill in coaching. Effective coaching is a high-level skill requiring the ability to identify performance problems, diagnose performance problems in terms of ability and motivation, give candid feedback, and jointly solve performance problems. It also requires the ability to ask good questions and to listen. Finally, it requires the personal attributes of empathy and patience. This is no small order. To some managers lacking in these skills, the easy way out is simply to exclude coaching from their job functions.

Lack of perceived reward for coaching. It is a truism that most managers will focus on those activities for which they believe they will be rewarded. The closer and tighter the linkage between the activity and the reward, the greater the effort expended. This is simple reinforcement theory that most people learn in Psychology 101. With regard to coaching, the problem is that many managers do not perceive any relation between their efforts in coaching their staff and the size of the monetary reward they receive at year-end. Hence, the manager asks: "Why should I devote a substantial portion of my time to coaching my staff if I get no reward for it?" This same manager then goes on to say: "If I devote the same amount of time to activities that contribute directly to my department's bottom line, then I will see the reward." To rebut this view, higher level managers will reply that there is indeed a connection between amount of time devoted to coaching and the figures on the bottom line. This may very well be true, but we are discussing here the lack of *perceived* reward.

Being threatened by a potential replacement. In terms of pure logic, it makes good sense that every manager should be developing one or more backups for his or her position. Such a state of affairs would mean that the manager is gaining in power and is in a better position to be considered for a promotion. If we go beyond the domain of logic to that of emotion, we become aware of a serious obstacle. Here we find our arational manager obsessed with the fear that he or she could be replaced — *and by someone whom he or she trained*. It hardly seems fair. For this reason, many managers go on their way creating the illusion that they are irreplaceable. If they were not in their present positions, the organization would surely collapse.

These are serious obstacles to being a developmental manager. No one of them should be minimized. But the leader-manager who is genuinely committed to being a developmental manager can overcome these obstacles, and the rewards may be beyond what one can even imagine.

SUCCESS THROUGH THE ACCOMPLISHMENT OF OTHERS

Suppose that you had the responsibility for evaluating a given manager's effectiveness over the past year. Suppose further that you had to restrict your assessment to one particular measure that would reflect how this person performed as a manager. What measure would you select?

There are so many possibilities: dollar volume, net profit, overhead costs, average product cost, number of new customers, accident rates per shift, percent of voluntary staff turnover, acquisition of new staff, acquistion of new equipment, measures of staff morale, and on and on. I am sure that you could add other possible measures, depending on the nature of your business.

Which measure would you choose? You are restricted to one.

The real measure of a leader-manager's effectiveness is pinpointed by Lawrence Appley:

> The real measure of the effectiveness of leadership is what is actually happening to the individuals directly responsible to that leadership — what changes are really taking place in the climate of the workplace, in the caliber of the people, and in the relationships of supervisor and supervised. (*Management in Action*, p. 109)

This is a beautiful observation. It captures a key function of leadership. We can gauge leadership in terms of *what is actually happening to the individuals directly responsible to that leadership*. If nothing is happening to these individuals, then we have an absence of leadership. But if these individuals are learning, growing, and taking on greater responsibilities, then we are witnessing leadership at its best.

To make this issue somewhat more concrete, let's consider the management styles of two different middle-level managers. Joe and Jodi are department managers working in the same organization. Each has four section managers as direct reports and is responsible for about 100 people. But here the similarity ends. They are radically different in their management styles.

Joe takes pride in *achieving results*. He is a hard-driving workaholic who will do whatever is necessary to achieve his annual performance objectives. Working 16-hour days at least six days each week, Joe does the work of at least two people. He attempts to push his people fairly hard. But if they can't fulfill his expectations, then he will do their work for them. He doesn't mind "taking their monkeys"— if that's what's required to get the job done. To Joe, the job of management is *getting results*.

Taking stock at the end of the year, we must agree that some of Joe's accomplishments are impressive. The dollar volume for his department was up 25% over the previous year, his net profit exceeded goal by 20%, and overhead expenses were reduced by 15%. Anyone interested only in the bottom line would have to be impressed with Joe's accomplishments.

In the "softer" areas, however, there is reason for concern. When we look at Joe's people, for instance, we see that they haven't grown over the past year. They essentially are performing at about the same level at which they were performing 12 months previously. They work reasonably hard, but they aren't stretching. They all know full well that if they can't accomplish a given task, then Joe will do it for them. Joe is a Lone Ranger *par excellence*.

Jodi is radically different in her approach to management. She takes pride in *building a team* that can achieve results. She works with her team in developing annual departmental objectives and strategies for achieving those objectives. She then meets with each of her direct reports on an individual basis to agree on specific performance objectives. After this is accomplished, she turns her attention to *helping her people achieve their objectives*. To this end, she helps remove roadblocks, helps obtain the needed resources, and *coaches*. Every meeting with one of her staff is viewed as an opportunity for coaching. Jodi is a developmental manager *par excellence*.

To assess Jodi's performance, it is necessary to consider her attainments in both bottom-line financial performance and staff development. (Other areas, of course, would be considered, but for purposes of illustration, we will look at only these two.) In terms of bottom-line results, Jodi was right on target: She achieved her objectives on dollar volume, net profit, and overhead expenses. Here we would evaluate her as "good." But in terms of staff development, we would evaluate her as "exceptional." Each one of her direct reports has grown substantially in knowledge, skills, and taking on broader responsibilities. What is most impressive is that each one of these direct reports is serving as an effective developmental manager for each of his or her people. What is rather subtle here—and could easily be missed—is that Jodi is having a multiplier effect on the entire department. By serving as an excellent role model as a developmental manager, she is having a tremendous impact on the growth and development of 100 people.

If we based our evaluations of these two managers only on bottom-line financial performance, we would be inclined to give Joe a higher rating than Jodi. But what if we evaluated them on *total* performance, which includes building for the future? Then surely we would be inclined to give Jodi the higher rating.

As we consider the case study of these two managers, it is worthwhile to reflect on the century-old definition of management: "getting things done through others." It is agreed that Joe is getting things done, but not necessarily through others. He does it himself. But Jodi, in her role as a developmental manager, is truly functioning in accord with this classical view of management. Thus, we would give Joe a high rating as an individual contributor but only a marginal rating as a manager. With regard to Jodi, we would give her an outstanding rating as a manager, and especially as a developmental manager. As for any side bets on who will achieve the greater success in the long run, I'll bet on Jodi.

If you agree with me in my wager, then surely you will agree with Lawrence Appley when he says:

> If you want the people below you in your organization to derive genuine satisfaction from the achievement of their subordinates, place great emphasis upon the work that is done under their supervision. Ask for the accomplishments of a manager in terms of the accomplishments of his people. Appraise him on the quality of their work and reward him for what they do. Take the emphasis off personal production, and, in all probability, credit will be given where credit is due. (*Management in Action*, p. 144)

ATTRIBUTES OF THE DEVELOPMENTAL MANAGER

Developmental managers have a number of characteristics that distinguish them from nondevelopmental managers. The following are 10 key attributes of the developmental manager. You may find it worthwhile to evaluate yourself on them.

Gets great satisfaction in helping others grow. Many managers enjoy seeing *themselves* grow, and there is nothing at all wrong with that. A smaller number of managers, however, derive genuine satisfaction from helping *others* grow. Effective leader-managers take a personal interest in the development of each of their staff. They help remove barriers, they help obtain resources, and they provide effective coaching. Witnessing the growth and development of their people gives them great joy. The feeling that one has contributed to another person's growth is a reward in and of itself.

Views development of staff as a major job function. Some managers view coaching as a luxury. If all of their primary duties are taken care of, and they have time to spare, then they might devote some time to coaching. Staff development simply is not perceived as a core activity. Not so with developmental managers. These managers place coaching right in the core of their job functions. They consider coaching to be just as important as any of the other job functions, and they are willing to be held accountable for how well they develop their people. In fact, they evaluate their own performance on the basis of how much their people are learning, growing, and expanding in job responsibilities.

Views individuals in terms of their potential. Many managers view their people only in terms of what they are or what they have been. Somewhat rare are those managers who view their individual staff members in terms of their potential, but this is exactly what developmental managers do. They perceive both actuality and potentiality. They confirm individual jobholders on the basis of both what they are and what they might become. And they delight in helping to convert potentiality into actuality — to help their people become what they can become.

Has high expectations for each staff member. Being a developmental manager is neither a wishy-washy approach nor a mushy approach. On the contrary, it is a tough approach. Developmental managers have high expectations for themselves and for their people. They communicate clear expectations to their team as a whole and to each individual member of the team. By creating a climate that promotes higher levels of achievement, they convey the message that each member of the team is expected to continue learning, growing, and expanding in job responsibilities. The manager will serve as a facilitator in the process, but each member is expected to assume the primary responsibility for his or her own development. Every member of the team is expected to make a commitment to lifelong learning.

Builds on the strengths of individual staff members. Unfortunately, some managers focus only on the weaknesses of their individual staff members. It is as though they have a template or model of the ideal job holder and then evaluate each of their people in the light of the model. Discrepancies are noted and then brought to the attention of the jobholder. In sharp contrast, developmental managers focus on the *strengths* of their people. They realize that no one is perfect — including themselves. And they realize that they are not in the business of creating clones of themselves. Thus, they know from experience that a far more effective approach to staff development is to identify the particular strengths of each of their people and then help enhance these strengths. Each person is prized for his or her uniqueness and the special contribution that the person can make to the whole.

Is able to diagnose performance problems. To be an effective developmental manager, it is important to be able to diagnose performance problems. If an employee's performance is found lacking, it may be no easy task to identify the causal factor (or factors). It may be a problem of lack of skill; it may be a problem of lack of motivation; it may be a problem associated with system design; or it may be a combination of two or even three of these problems. Through careful observation and questioning, the perceptive manager will be able to discern which of these causal factors is paramount in a given situation. And as the sages have told us, "A problem clearly defined is already half solved."

Takes mistakes in stride, so long as the individual learns from them. Anyone who has ever worked in an environment in which mistakes are not tolerated understands the negative impact of such an environment. People simply will not risk; they are reluctant to make decisions; and they are fearful of delegating. Certainly, an environment in which mistakes are tolerated would be more innovative — and productive. As one observer has noted, "Show me a person who says he never makes mistakes and I will show you a person who never makes decisions." We know from experience that anyone who makes decisions will make some mistakes. No one can be expected to bat 100%. The important thing is that people learn from their mistakes.

Takes a forward-looking approach in dealing with problems. Whenever managers are informed that a problem has arisen because a mistake was made, two different types of responses will be noted. At one extreme, we will see the response of "Who made the mistake?

Who is to blame?" At the other extreme, we will see the response of "What is the problem? What can we do to fix it?" The first approach is *maladaptive*: it is simply finger-pointing, looking for a scapegoat. The second is *adaptive*: it focuses on solving the problem. The developmental manager takes an adaptive approach in dealing with problems.

Is authentic in giving feedback. An essential ingredient of learning is effective feedback. If the feedback is either deceptive or nonexistent, learning will suffer. It is essential that you give your people candid feedback on their performance. You must deal with both the positives and the negatives. If you avoid, or even delay, the negatives, you are hurting both your people and yourself. Bear in mind that you are showing the other person respect if you convey the belief that he or she is mature enough to accept constructive negative feedback.

Is a good listener. To help your people grow and develop, you must be a very good listener. You must be able to listen actively; you must be able to listen without evaluating; you must be able to listen to both words and feelings; and you must be able to hear both what is said and what is not said. Easy to say, difficult to do. But if you can master the art of active listening, you may discover that you have acquired an essential skill for being a developmental manager.

These are 10 important attributes of the developmental manager. How did you fare in the self-assessment? If you have identified some specific areas for improvement, and are committed to working on them, I say, "That's great! Then do it."

TO BECOME A DEVELOPMENT MANAGER

Assuming that you want to become a developmental manager, what might you do? There is no single panacea, and there are no simple cookbook answers. But the collective experience of a number of successful leader-managers has generated some practical guidelines.

1. **Take a personal interest in the development of each of your staff.**
    To be a developmental manager, you must get to know your people as individual persons. What are their life goals? What are their career goals? What do they consider to be their major

developmental needs? In the typical organizational environment
with the rush of day-to-day activities, a serious discussion of such
questions may be difficult or even impossible. For this reason, a
manager of my acquaintance found an effective solution by arranging informal lunchtime meetings with each of his direct
reports. With four supervisors reporting to him, he has lunch with
one of them each week. The cycle is then repeated each month.
He finds that these meetings are invaluable to him in establishing
and maintaining a personal relationship with each of his people.

2. **Communicate clear expectations to each of your people.** For
   employees to perform well and to continue to learn and grow,
   they need to know what is expected of them. They need to know
   their job functions, their specific performance objectives, the standards of performance, and the criteria on which they will be
   evaluated. Past research studies have shown that the percentage
   of overlap between the job incumbent's perception of his or her
   job requirements and the immediate supervisor's perception is
   only about 50%. The problem obviously is one of communication. Don't let this happen to you.

3. **Provide your staff with the tools they need to do their jobs.** It
   is frustrating to employees when they lack specific tools that would
   allow them to be more effective and more efficient in their jobs.
   Their job performance undoubtedly will suffer, and, more than
   likely, the productivity of the unit will suffer. It is incumbent on
   you to stay abreast of the tools that are needed by your people
   and how to go about getting them. Be it a word processor, a personal computer, or a computer software package, you must make
   a conscientious effort to obtain the tools that are needed by your
   staff. Granted, limited budgets frequently are a barrier. Nevertheless, through cost-effectiveness analyses, you must be able to
   convince your management that such purchases are justified.

4. **Help remove obstacles.** It is my impression that there are large
   numbers of self-motivated employees who are demotivated in their
   work because of the barriers associated with the organization's
   bureaucratic structure. Without the barriers, they could perform
   well. But because of the barriers, their performance is significantly
   diminished. They simply need someone to help run interference
   for them. As a leader-manager, this is your job. Be it getting an

approval from a particular manager, prompting upper management to act on a needed decision, or even expediting an important purchase order, you might be in a far better position to deal with the matter than your staff member. Deciding when to intervene requires considerable judgment on your part: Don't take your people's "monkeys" when the monkeys clearly should rest with them.

5. **Be an effective delegator.** Delegation and coaching should go hand-in-hand. Proper delegation involves coaching, and effective coaching involves delegation. Poor indeed is the practice of simply assigning a new task to a junior staff member and then implying that "I'll meet you at the pass upon completion of the assignment." Rather than delegation, such an approach might better be described as abdication. A well thought out approach to delegation has been laid out by William Dyer. As shown in Figure 25, Dyer's approach points up the close linkage between delegation and coaching. As you review this strategy, you might be inclined to think that such an approach would demand a considerable amount of your time. And you are correct — at least *up front*. But if carried out properly, the strategy should yield a substantial long-term time savings.

6. **Provide effective day-to-day coaching.** Coaching should not be limited to the formal performance reviews and the eye-catching situations resulting from mistakes made by staff. The alert manager will see and seize upon many opportunities to coach on a day-to-day basis. These opportunities may range from discussing a specific job assignment to simply being asked a question by one of your staff. Whenever these situations arise, ask yourself: "Is this an opportunity for me to help this person grow?" And be mindful of Confucius' admonition that "The ideal teacher guides his students, but does not take them to the place."

7. **Encourage your staff members to reach out in new directions.** It is very easy for people to get locked into their "comfort zones" and remain there. These are the spheres in which they have confidence they can perform well because they have resided there for such a long time. In a rapidly changing environment, such restrictive behavior ultimately leads to obsolescence. Don't let this happen to your people. Encourage them to reach out in new

1. Identify the assignment, project, or area of work that is to be delegated.

2. Identify the appropriate person to whom the work will be delegated.

3. Discuss the proposed task to be delegated with the one who is proposed to do it.

4. Make sure the person doing the task has the appropriate resources (time, money, equipment, assistance, etc.) and necessary authority to do the work.

5. Provide the needed training, orientation, or direction the person may need to do the delegated activity.

6. Allow the person to move ahead with strong support, encouragement, and positive reinforcement.

7. Agree in advance on times to review progress.

8. Upon completion of the task, critique the total experience.

From *Contemporary Issues in Management and Organizational Development*, by W. Dyer, 1983, p. 62. Reprinted with permission of Addison-Wesley Publishing Co., Reading, MA.

Figure 25.   A strategy for effective delegation.

directions. Encourage them to expand their jobs. Encourage them
to take on new job assignments and new projects. Encourage them
to acquire new knowledge and skills. Encourage them to create
new visions. Most important: be a good role model.

8. **Conduct effective performance appraisals.** One of the complaints
that I hear most frequently in management seminars is dissatisfac-
tion with the organization's performance appraisal program. Even
if the organization has established a reasonably good performance
appraisal program, many seminar participants complain that
their immediate supervisors do not take the program seriously.
Here there is a clear message: Do not give performance appraisal
a short shift. Take it seriously. Bear in mind that the primary
purpose of performance appraisal is the *improvement of job performance*. This is a goal that you and each of your staff members
should have in common. View the formal performance appraisal
interview as an excellent opportunity for coaching, an opportunity
to review the past accomplishments, to discuss a person's strengths
and areas in need of improvement, and to agree upon specific
performance objectives for the next review period. Such an approach to performance appraisal will reap large dividends.

9. **Be a good helper in career planning.** As mentioned previously,
the individual job holder should assume the primary responsibility
for his or her own career planning. But, as a manager, this does
not let you "off the hook." You should be an active and interested
facilitator in the process. In a paper entitled "Improving Professional Development by Applying the Four-Stage Career Model,"
Thompson, Baker, and Smallwood have laid out a realistic division of responsibilities for the employee and the manager. Reviewing and reflecting on the guidelines shown in Figure 26 should
help you define your responsibilities in career planning.

10. **Help others become leaders.** Perhaps your greatest challenge as
a leader-manager is to help others become leaders. This is one
of the principal areas that distinguishes the developmental manager from the Lone Ranger. The masked rider has only Tonto,
who is expected to remain a follower. But you, as a developmental
manager, should view your people as potential leaders. You can
help them become leaders by providing appropriate job oppor-

tunities and by providing effective coaching. The essential requirement on your part, of course, is commitment.

Implementing this plan of action obviously will require from you
a great deal of time and effort. Most important, it will require *ongoing
commitment*. But the ensuing reward in the form of a more capable
staff will make the effort worthwhile.

Dimension	Professional Employee	Manager
Responsibility	Assumes responsibility for individual career development.	Assumes responsibility for employee development.
Information	Obtains career information through self-evaluation and data collection. What do I enjoy doing? Where do I want to go?	Provides information by holding up a mirror of reality: How manager views the employee. How others view the employee. How "things work around here."
Planning	Develops an individual plan to reach objectives.	Helps employee assess plan.
Follow-through	Invites management support through high performance on the current job, by understanding the scope of the job and taking appropriate initiative.	Provides coaching and relevant information on opportunities.

From "Improving Professional Development by Applying the Four-Stage Career Model," by Thompson, Baker and
Smallwood, *Organizational Dynamics*, 1986, p. 59. Reprinted with permission of The American Management Association,
New York, NY.

Figure 26.   A realistic division of responsibilities in career discussions.

BENEFITS OF BEING A DEVELOPMENTAL MANAGER

In their book, Managing for Excellence , Bradford and Cohen stress that the Manager-as-Developer model is basically a tough approach:

> It is tough in setting high standards (and holding people to them). It is tough in requiring that the manager hold subordinates' feet to the fire when they may want to avoid the difficult issues. It is tough in pushing for conflicts to be identified and worked through rather than smoothed over. It is tough in requiring that people be confronted (rather than shunted aside, or ignored) when they don't come through. And it is tough in demanding that the manager be willing to be open to confrontation as well. [p. 287]

Indeed, there is nothing wishy-washy or mushy about being a developmental manager. It is a tough approach.

If you are willing to implement this tough approach in a faithful manner, you are almost certain to realize a number of benefits.

A more capable staff. By making a genuine commitment to being a developmental manager, you will have a more capable staff. If you have done a good job in recruiting and selecting your people, then you will have a staff with high potential. Some of this potential can be transformed into actuality simply through job assignments and self-learning. To really make the most of the potential, however, your attention to coaching is needed. For a given staff member, your commitment to coaching can make the difference between an annual performance rating of B − and one of A + . This is no small achievement.

An attitude of lifelong learning among your staff. One of the exciting things about being a developmental manager is that you create an environment that promotes lifelong learning. The external world, technology, and the organization are all continually changing. It is essential that your people stay abreast of these changes and be able to cope with them. Your continuing stress on staff development will convey the message to your staff that lifelong learning should be accepted as a "way of life."

Higher self-esteem among staff. An individual's self-esteem is partly a function of his or her perceived worth to the organization and to society at large. If a person plateaus on the learning curve at an early age, then the self-perception of worth is diminished. But if a person continues to learn, to grow, and to expand in job responsibilities, then the self-perception of worth is enhanced. By being a developmental manager, you have the power to influence the self-esteem of your staff.

Higher motivation and job satisfaction among your staff. The learning curve for many jobs levels off somewhere between six to twelve months on the job. If the jobholder remains in the same job for several more years with no growth in knowledge and skills, the performance curve is very likely to decline. As you know, the reason for the decline is boredom. By being a developmental manager, you will be able to help each person's learning curve continue to rise, which will prevent boredom and bring about higher levels of motivation and job satisfaction.

A multiplier effect. If you are an effective developmental manager, then the people reporting to you are likely to emulate you in their relationships with their staff. They too will become developmental managers. To your credit, you will have promoted a positive attitude toward continual staff development. Further, you will have demonstrated the skills necessary for being a developmental manager. What better way could your people learn how to become effective developmental managers?

A reputation as a developmental manager. In most organizations, the true developmental managers seem to "stand out." The reason for this is that they are so rare. Far too many managers restrict their attention to bottom-line financial performance and reacting to the immediate needs of the day. They simply "don't have time to coach their staff." If you are able to attend to these immediate concerns while at the same time devoting sufficient time to coaching your staff, you will earn a reputation as a developmental manager. As a consequence, you will be able to attract high-potential people to your work unit. Further, you will be noticed in a positive way by upper-level managers, especially by those who have a long-range view of the organization's success.

Greater productivity. Collectively, the above benefits are almost certain to lead to greater productivity for your work unit. Your concerted effort toward being an effective developmental manager should lead to a more capable staff, an environment that promotes lifelong learning, a staff with high self-esteem, a staff with high motivation, several direct reports who also are developmental managers, and the ability to attract high-potential people. No small achievement! It can not be guaranteed, but the probability that these benefits will result in greater productivity is extremely high.

The benefits of being a developmental manager are clear. Are there disadvantages? I can think of only one: You may lose a large number of people to other departments. You may be developing your people more rapidly than your work unit can absorb them into higher-level positions, and they are recruited by other departments. Even so, this should not distress you. An enlightened upper-level management should be keeping score and giving you credit for your accomplishments as a developmental manager.

As a final note, it is important to appreciate that being a developmental manager is empowerment at its best. By helping your people expand their capabilities, you are giving them more power. As a consequence, you will have more power. As one side of the coin expands, so does the other side.

X

Measuring

To be a good judge is to have a sense of the relative indicative
or signifying values of the various features of the perplexing situation; to know what to let go of as of no account;
what to eliminate as irrelevant; what to retain as conducive
to the outcome; what to emphasize as a clue to the difficulty.

John Dewey
How We Think

---

*A Strategy for Measuring • Understanding the Nature of the System • Focus
on Critical Success Factors • The Management Information System •
Managing by Walking Around • Coordinated Problem Solving*

A STRATEGY FOR MEASURING

The leader-manager frequently asks: "How are we doing?" A plan
for moving from the present state toward the desired state has been
set in motion, and the manager wants to know if things are progressing
according to the plan. If an accurate answer to the question is not
forthcoming, the manager may end up someplace where he or she
does not want to be.

To measure progress, the manager periodically must answer three
basic questions:

1. What information do I need?
2. How do I go about getting the information?
3. What do I do with the information once I get it?

Proposing a strategy for answering these three questions is the purpose of this chapter. The key feature of the strategy is that it is a blend of "high tech" and "high touch." With high tech representing the technological dimension of management and high touch representing the human dimension, the proposed strategy offers a *balanced approach* to measuring progress.

In the book, *Megatrends*, John Naisbitt puts the high-tech/high-touch issue in perspective:

> High tech/high touch is a formula I use to describe the way we have responded to technology. What happens is that whenever new technology is introduced into society, there must be a counterbalancing human response — that is, *high touch* — or the technology is rejected. The more the high tech, the more high touch.
>
> Now, at the dawn of the twenty-first century, high tech/high touch has truly come of age. Technology and our human potential are the two great challenges and adventures facing humankind today. The great lesson we must learn from the principles of high tech/high touch is a modern version of the ancient Greek ideal — *balance*.
>
> *We must learn to balance the material wonders of technology with the spiritual demands of our human nature.* [pp. 39-40]

This perspective provided by Naisbitt serves as the underlying rationale for the strategy shown in Figure 27. Included in this strategy for measuring progress are five interrelated steps: (1) understanding the nature of the system, (2) focus on critical success factors, (3) establishment of a management information system, (4) managing by walking around, and (5) coordinated problem solving. Each step is essential to the success of the strategy.

The first step in the strategy is to understand the nature of the system. To the extent that any organization is an assemblage of interrelated elements directed toward common goals, it may be considered a system. There are cause-and-effect relations throughout the system, what may be called "if-then" relations. It is essential that the manager understand these if-then relations.

A clear understanding of the nature of the system should lead to identification of critical success factors. These are the five to eight factors that will determine the success or failure of the system. It

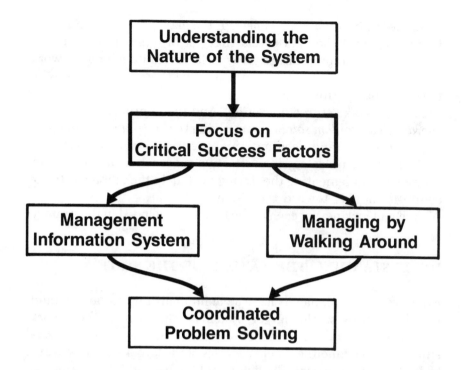

Figure 27. A strategy for measuring.

is important that the manager pinpoint these factors and ascertain what type of information is needed to measure their status.

One way to collect information on the status of the critical success factors is through the establishment of a formal management information system. Typically, this would be a computer-based system that provides the manager with data on either a regularly scheduled or as-needed basis. Here the manager would be looking at "hard" data such as expenditures, revenue, net profit, etc.

A second way to collect information on the critical success factors is through managing by walking around, or, in the vernacular of Tom Peters, "MBWA." This would involve the manager in interacting with employees and customers on a face-to-face basis. Here the manager would be collecting "soft" data on such factors as attitudes, feelings, motivation, etc. It is important to appreciate that the effective leader-manager places as much weight on the "soft" data as on the "hard" data.

Once the information is collected, the manager must decide what to do with it. If the data reveal that performance is according to plan, it may be appropriate to give special recognition for good work. On the other hand, if the data indicate that there are deviations between actual performance and desired performance, it may be necessary to take corrective action. And the approach called for is *coordinated problem solving* — involving the key players in diagnosing the problem and deciding on appropriate corrective action.

This five-step strategy is an effective approach to measuring performance. Implementing the strategy will help the manager stay on course in moving toward the vision.

We will look next at each of the five steps included in the strategy.

UNDERSTANDING THE NATURE OF THE SYSTEM

Effective leader-managers have a common affinity for understanding the nature of the larger system within which they work. Whenever they take on new job assignments, they make a special effort to understand the inner workings of the larger system of which their work unit is a part. Realizing that the needed information can not be uncovered simply from printed documents, they are relentless in their probing. They observe, inquire, and integrate until they are satisfied that they have a valid conceptual model of the system.

John Dewey, the philosopher and educator, was astute in his portrayal of the "good judge." This is a person "who has a sense of the relative indicative or signifying values of the various features of the perplexing situation; knows what to let go of as of no account; what to eliminate as irrelevant; what to retain as conducive to the outcome; what to emphasize as a clue to the difficulty." In essence, this is a person who has a profound understanding of the larger system within which he or she works.

In *The Human Organization*, Rensis Likert stresses that the manager should have a good grasp of two aspects of the system: the *nature* of the system and the *state* of the system. In this regard, he likens the manager's job to that of the physician:

> A physician needs two different kinds of information to make a correct diagnosis. First, he must know a great deal about the nature of human beings. This knowledge is based on extensive research which relates symptoms to causes and

measurements of body conditions to the health of the organism, thereby revealing the character of the human body's
normal and abnormal functioning. This knowledge gives
the doctor insights into how the system ought to function,
so that he can know what he needs to measure and how
he needs to interpret the measurements. The second kind
of information needed by the doctor to discover the patient's
state of health at any particular time is that revealed by the
appropriate measurements and tests made on that patient
at that time. [p. 128]

It is generally understood that measurement of progress is dependent on accurately assessing the *state* of the system at any point in
time. It also must be understood that accurately assessing the state
of the system is dependent on understanding the *nature* of the system.

To understand the nature of the system, Likert stresses that the
manager must grasp the relations between and among three types
of variables:

1. **Causal variables:** independent variables that determine the
   course of developments within an organization and the results
   achieved by the organization.
2. **Intervening variables:** mediating variables that reflect the internal state and health of the organization.
3. **End-result variables:** the dependent variables that reflect the
   achievements of the organization.

As an illustration of how these three classes of variables inter-
relate, we can consider the example of the effect of leadership style
on productivity. In many situations, it would be assumed that a participative leadership style would be more effective than an autocratic
style. This premise can be tested by correlating leadership style (causal
variable) with employee motivation (intervening variable), and then
correlating employee motivation with productivity (end-result variable). In this way it could be demonstrated that leadership style has
an effect on productivity, but *via* employee motivation.

Given this framework for "understanding the nature of the system," we will illustrate the notion by considering the dollar flow in
a for-profit engineering firm. You may not have any particular interest in an engineering firm, but the principles elucidated here would
apply to any type of organization.

The dollar flow of the illustrative firm is shown in Figure 28. We

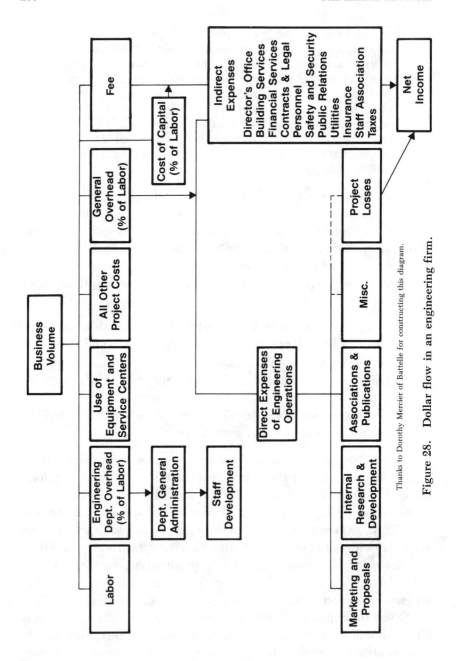

Thanks to Dorothy Mercier of Battelle for constructing this diagram.

Figure 28.   Dollar flow in an engineering firm.

will consider the business volume to be the causal variable, the net income to be the end-result variable, and everything else to be intervening variables.

The business volume is broken down into these categories: labor, use of equipment and service centers, all other project costs, overhead (engineering department overhead, general overhead, and cost of capital), and fee. The general overhead is apportioned as direct expenses of engineering operations (funds allocated to the engineering departments) and indirect expenses (funds used to operate the company as a whole).

Effective managers understand the causal relations in this financial system. For example, they realize that increasing labor (time on projects) by one percent can have at least a 10-percent impact on net income. They realize that a two-percent overrun in project losses can cause a 20-percent decrease in net income. Further, they realize that a fee increase of three percent can have a 30-percent impact on net income. These multiplier effects are indeed noteworthy, and they are ever-present in the mind of the effective manager.

Managers who understand this financial system also realize that it presents them with a number of important decisions. For example, will the return-on-investment with the marketing and proposals funds be better in the industrial arena or in the government arena? With the funds allocated for internal research and development, is it better to invest in a small number of really good ideas or in a large number of possibly promising ideas? With the funds for associations and publications, which particular associations and publications should be pursued? These are important questions, and the answers generated will determine the success or failure of the manager.

There are numerous other examples of important causal relations in the system, but these will illustrate the point that for you to be able to measure your unit's progress, *it is essential that you understand the inner workings of the larger system.*

FOCUS ON CRITICAL SUCCESS FACTORS

I recall reading an enlightening article about a feisty vice-president of public relations in a large industrial organization. This manager had become troubled by the number of printed reports being distributed on a regular basis to all managers throughout the organization. He felt that the number of reports was far greater than what was actually needed by these managers.

To determine which reports were actually needed, the vice president conducted an experiment. For one month he *stopped the distribution* of all internal reports. He then obtained feedback from the managers. He found some noteworthy results. One-third of the reports were claimed to be essential to the work of the managers. Another third of the reports were not really needed, but a number of managers were simply curious about what had happened to them. With regard to the final third, *no one even inquired.* Certainly, this little experiment provides an important message to all managers, and especially those responsible for distributing reports to other managers.

It is informative to note how managers' perceptions of their information needs have changed over time. In the early 1970s managers were calling for more information in the form of reports, computer printouts, meetings, etc. But by the mid-1980s many of these same managers were crying "Enough!" They were getting *too much information.*

In his book, *The Art of Problem Solving*, Russell Ackoff makes special note of the problem of information overload:

> It is common knowledge that most managers suffer from information overload; therefore, providing them with additional information, even relevant information, can help little because they do not have the time required to separate the wheat from the chaff. [pp. 202–203]

If we simply try to maximize the amount of information that we provide managers, we undoubtedly will create "noise" in the system. Daniel Katz and Robert Kahn state it well when they say:

> In terms of information theory, unrestricted communication produces noise in the system. Without patterning, without pause, without precision, there is sound but there is no music. Without structure, without spacing, without specification, there is a Babel of tongues but there is no meaning. (*The Social Psychology of Organizations*, p. 430)

During the past decade or so, we have learned a great deal about meeting the information needs of managers. One of the most significant things learned, and something that now appears obvious, is that the relation between the amount of data provided to managers and the quality of their performance is not linear. Rather, as shown in

Figure 29, the relation is curvilinear. Initially, there is a linear relation between the amount of data provided to managers and their performance, but, with increasing amounts of data being provided, performance levels off and then declines. Thus, what began as a positive effect turns into a negative effect because eventually the managers are burdened with "data overload."

In his classic paper, "Information Input, Overload, and Psychopathology," J. G. Miller has documented the consequences of information overload:

1. Omission — failing to handle some of the input.
2. Error — processing information incorrectly.
3. Filtering — neglecting to process certain types of information.
4. Queuing — letting things pile up until a later date.
5. Approximation — lowering standards of precision.
6. Multiple channels — delegating information processing to others.
7. Escape — refusing to handle the input at all.

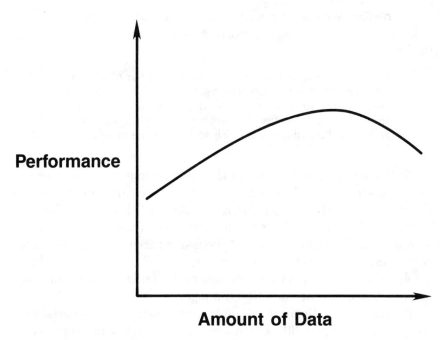

Figure 29.   Relation between amount of data and performance.

Most of us can relate to many, and perhaps all, of these quandaries. They are real, and they clearly point up the problem of information overload.

The rather obvious solution to the information-overload problem is to focus on the important variables. Any manager can collect data on scores of variables, but the key is to identify the salient ones. Rensis Likert places the issue in perspective:

> Only the most important variables which have the most marked relationships and which best summarize many other variables need be reported to each operating unit. Each manager and his department need data on only a relatively few dimensions, namely, those which are operationally most important. This would conserve time and focus attention on matters having the greatest influence on the department's performance. (*The Human Organization*, p. 144)

Consistent with this perspective provided by Likert, the information specialists have formulated an effective method for focusing on the most important variables. This is the critical-success-factor process described in Chapter V.

To review what was presented previously, we will again present the definition of critical success factors as offered by Bullen and Rockart:

> Critical success factors are the limited number of areas in which satisfactory results will insure successful competitive performance for the individual, department, or organization. CSFs are the few key areas where "things must go right" for the business to flourish and for the manager's goals to be attained. [p. 7]

Bullen and Rockart point out that most managers spend a great deal of their time both at work and in their leisure time thinking about those specific areas of activity that are "close to the bone." Much time is spent thinking about ways to improve performance in each of these areas. Granted that these areas are implicit, the value of the CSF process is to make them *explicit*. Through a procedure involving in-depth interviewing, information specialists are able to identify the CSFs for each line manager.

Examples of critical success factors for a specific managerial job are shown in Figure 30. These are the CSFs for a manager of a research department at Battelle. There is one CSF for each of the eight Battelle values presented in Chapter V. A manager who performs well in all eight of these areas undoubtedly will have a successful department.

To "get a handle" on the meaning and significance of critical success factors, I encourage you to reflect on the job positions listed in Figure 31. These are the major areas of responsibility in a large manufacturing firm. What do you think would be the principal

1. Develops and markets programs that will help solve *significant societal problems*.

2. Hires *innovative* staff member and establishes an environment that fosters innovation.

3. Establishes standards and procedures to assure that all work is of *high quality*.

4. Through words and actions encourages and achieves effective *teamwork*.

5. Develops and implements a long-range plan that will generate continual *viability* and *growth*.

6. Provides the resources and encouragement needed by the staff to participate in *professional* and *community activities*.

7. Communicates crystal-clear expectations regarding *integrity*.

8. Makes effective use of resources to achieve both short-term and long-term *profitability*.

Figure 30.   Critical success factors for a department manager at Battelle.

critical success factors for each position? What are the five to eight areas in which satisfactory results will insure successful competitive performance? To check your answers, you may wish to talk with managers who are knowledgeable in these various areas.

Once you feel that you have a reasonably good grasp of the meaning of critical success factors, I encourage you to formulate the CSFs for your own work unit. The specification of the CSFs can then serve as the cornerstone for your measurement strategy.

In a large manufacturing firm, what would be the critical success factors for these positions?

- **Director of Manufacturing**

- **Director of Marketing/Sales**

- **Director of Research and Development**

- **Director of Engineering**

- **Director of Quality Assurance**

- **Director of Management Information Systems**

- **Director of Accounting and Finance**

- **Director of Facilities**

- **Director of Purchasing**

- **Director of Human Resources**

Figure 31.   Identification of critical success factors.

THE MANAGEMENT INFORMATION SYSTEM

Data on the status of critical success factors can be provided by an effective management information system. Today, information specialists have sufficient know-how and computer tools to establish an MIS to meet the specific information needs of each line manager. Here we see high-tech at its best.

Most organizations have established some type of formal management information system. Some of these systems are highly centralized, with all managers linked to the main-frame computer. Others are highly decentralized, with managers purchasing or designing software packages for their own personal computers. Still others have achieved what might be considered an optimal position on the centralization-decentralization continuum, which results in uniformity across the organization, while still meeting the unique needs of individual managers.

Some organizations have formalized the structure of the MIS component. This component may be headed by either a vice president or director who is charged with meeting the information needs of the entire enterprise. It is significant to note that, in recent years, the head of the MIS component has been given more resources and substantially greater authority.

From organization to organization, the quality of the MIS varies considerably. For the past several years I have been asking participants in management seminars to evaluate the MIS in their own organizations. Using a 10-point scale (with "10" being high), the resulting scores have ranged from "1" to "9." The low scores, "1" to "3," usually reveal that no one in the organization has been given the responsibility for establishing and maintaining an MIS. The high scores, say "8" or "9," indicate that it is indeed possible to design an MIS to meet the needs of individual managers.

Today we know a great deal about the features of an effective MIS. Building on the work of Bertram Colbert and others, I have formulated 10 key attributes of an effective MIS.

1. **Is tailored to job positions.** The information needs of a project manager are different from those of a department manager. The information needs of a department manager are different from those of a director. And the information needs of a director are

different from those of a president. An effective MIS will be designed to meet the unique needs of managers at different levels in the organization.

2. **Is tailored to the needs of individual managers.** One manager needs cost data only monthly; another needs these data at least weekly. One manager needs detailed data; another needs only summary data. One manager needs historical data; another needs futuristic projections. An effective MIS will be designed to meet the special needs of these individual managers.

3. **Provides data on critical success factors.** The easy way out is to simply give all managers data on all variables included in the MIS. But we know that this approach will result in a data overload for the managers. An effective MIS will provide each manager with data on the critical success factors that have been identified for his or her work unit — on the limited number of factors that will insure successful competitive performance.

4. **Reports to each level of management only the degree of detail needed.** In most organizations, we find that the degree of detail needed in MIS reports varies inversely with position level. Project managers, for example, need highly detailed cost reports. On the other hand, the department manager who is responsible for monitoring the projects in his or her department needs to receive only summary cost data on each project. An effective MIS will vary the amount of detail according to the level of each manager.

5. **Provides accurate data.** The people in the field of general semantics make a sharp distinction between "maps" and "territory." Maps are words and symbols, whereas the territory is concrete reality. In a similar way, we can say that the maps are the data provided by the MIS, and the territory is what is actually happening with regard to the critical success factors. An effective MIS will assure a high degree of congruence between the maps and the territory.

6. **Provides timely data.** I once met two managers from the same government agency who had different perceptions of their agency's management information system. One manager stated that the MIS provided cost data to the managers each month. His colleague then retorted, "Yes, but the data are three months

old!" A different perception indeed. In most cases, it is essential that managers receive data in a timely fashion.

7. **Presents data in a form that minimizes the need for analysis and interpretation.** Managers frequently complain that they must spend considerable amounts of time trying to organize the data provided to them by the MIS. Inasmuch as the data are presented in a very "raw" form, the manager is forced to organize the data in a form that will make it meaningful. This is a waste of the manager's time. It would be far more efficient if the MIS would organize and present the data in a form that would minimize the time required for analysis and interpretation.

8. **Prepares and presents data in a uniform manner.** To gauge their progress, most managers need to monitor trends — what is happening over time. Simply focusing on "point data" will not suffice. To this end, it is essential that the MIS present data in a uniform manner from one reporting period to the next. This will allow the manager to compare this month's performance (or this week's performance) with previous time intervals and then identify significant trends.

9. **Identifies, structures, and quantifies significant past relationships, and forecasts future relationships.** A project manager raises this question: "If our efficiency index for the second half of the project is the same as it was for the first half, what will be our financial status at the end of the project?" A department manager raises this question: "If our controllable expenses during the fourth quarter are 10 percent less than they were during the third quarter and our uncontrollable expenses remain the same, what will be the impact on the total annual budget?" An effective MIS can provide the answers.

10. **Appears to be cost-effective.** Information specialists have the knowledge and computer capabilities to design powerful management information systems. Indeed, the modern-day information specialist can design an MIS that is *effective*. The real challenge, however, is to design one that is *cost-effective*. The challenge is to design *a quality MIS at a reasonable cost*. This goal has been achieved by some organizations. And if something *is* being done, then it *can* be done.

Given these 10 features of a cost-effective MIS, you may find it beneficial to evaluate the MIS in your own organization. To what extent does this MIS *meet your particular needs?* Using a 5-point scale (with "5" being high), complete the evaluation scale presented in Figure 32. If your total score is 40 or greater, you should be pleased. But if you total score is 30 or less, you probably will agree that there is substantial room for improvement.

If the management information system in your organization does not meet your needs, don't be a Victim. Don't sit on the sidelines and complain that the information people are not responsive to your needs. Bear in mind that you are part of the management team.

---

5 = Excellent, 4 = Good, 3 = Satisfactory, 2 = Marginal, 1 = Poor

1. Is tailored to job positions.   _____

2. Is tailored to the needs of individual managers.   _____

3. Provides data on critical success factors.   _____

4. Reports to each level of management only the
    degree of detail needed.   _____

5. Provides accurate data.   _____

6. Provides timely data.   _____

7. Presents data in a form that minimizes the need
    for analysis and interpretation.   _____

8. Prepares and presents data in a uniform manner.   _____

9. Identifies, structures, and quantifies significant
    past relationships, and forecasts future
    relationships.   _____

10. Appears to be cost-effective.   _____

                                      Total score =   _____

Adapted from Bertram Colbert, "The Management Information System."

Figure 32.   Evaluate your management information system.

As a member of the management team, do whatever is reasonably possible to encourage the responsible parties to establish an MIS that will be responsive to your needs. You might even volunteer to head up a task force comprised of both line managers and information specialists to formulate the design requirements for an MIS that will meet the needs of all managers in the organization. Certainly, such a commitment will require a substantial amount of time on your part, but the long-term benefits surely will compensate you for the investment.

MANAGING BY WALKING AROUND

That managers should not rely solely on the management information system to gauge the progress of their work units has been stressed by Koontz, O'Donnell, and Weihrich:

> In any preoccupation with the devices of managerial control, one should never overlook the importance of control through personal observation. Budgets, charts, reports, ratios, auditors' recommendations, and other devices are essential to control. But the manager who relies wholly on these devices and sits, so to speak, in a soundproof control room reading dials and manipulating levers can hardly expect to do a thorough job of control. [pp. 759–60]

It is easy for managers to get "hooked" on the management information system as their sole means of measuring and controlling. The office with its computer terminal or personal computer provides a very secure setting, and the manager is in complete control. The manager can simply "call up" particular data, analyze it, interpret it, and then, via telephone or electronic mail, issue instructions for corrective action. In the confines of one's office, there are no personal confrontations and little wasted time. What a secure setting! Small wonder that many managers have little desire to leave their offices.

Tom Peters and his co-authors have made a significant contribution to the field of management through their emphasis on "managing by walking around"—or simply, MBWA. In both *In Search of Excellence* and *A Passion for Excellence*, the authors make special note of the importance of managing by walking around.

In *A Passion for Excellence*, Peters and Austin stress that MBWA means "being in touch":

> In our work with groups of all sorts we have commented time and again that we can make a strong case, which boils down to this: the number one managerial productivity problem in America is, quite simply, managers who are out of touch with their people and out of touch with their customers. And the alternative, "being in touch," doesn't come via computer printouts or the endless stream of overhead transparencies viewed in ten thousand darkened meeting rooms stretching across the continent. Being in touch means tangible, visceral ways of being informed.
>
> MBWA is being in touch, with customers, suppliers, your people. It facilitates innovation, and makes possible the teaching of values to every member of an organization. Listening, facilitating, and teaching and reinforcing values. What is this except leadership? [p. 8, p. 31]

After reflecting on the importance of MBWA, I had occasion to ask a department manager in a high-tech firm if he ever managed by walking around. His response to the question was revealing. He replied, "No. Because if I did, my people would think that I was snooping on them." What an interesting answer! I replied that, initially, his people might think that he was snooping on them, but if he did this frequently enough, they would begin to view his actions as a natural part of his job.

I also stressed to this manager that the important thing was how he went about the activity of managing by walking around. If he behaved as though he was simply snooping, then that is how his behavior would be viewed. On the other hand, if he acted in such a manner to suggest that he was interested in engaging in a genuine dialogue with his people, then his behavior undoubtedly would be viewed in a more positive light.

I once observed a manager of an automobile manufacturing plant who was very effective in his approach to managing by walking around. His rule for himself was to spend the mornings in the office and the afternoons on the plant floor.

On one particular afternoon, I had the opportunity to tour the plant with this plant manager. As he interacted with foremen and workers on a one-to-one basis, here were some of his questions: "How are you, Joe? Did the spare parts come in yesterday?" . . . "Hi, Bob. Thanks for getting those records over to me on time. Did you have any problem getting the information?" . . . "Hello, Frank. Did Jack get with you on that valve problem?" And so it went for the entire tour.

Several things impressed me on this tour. The plant manager knew every worker by name. More impressive was that he had first-hand knowledge of what was going on in the plant. It was clear that he knew the actual territory and did not rely simply on the maps. It also was clear that the workers did not view the plant manager's behavior as "snooping."

One of the keys to the effective use of MBWA is to not disrupt the organization's chain of command. Most managers would agree that the effective functioning of any organization depends on a reasonable chain of command. If the chain of command is too rigid, we witness a loss of initiative and creativity. If the chain of command is too loose, we find confusion and uncertainty. It seems evident that there must be a reasonable balance between freedom and structure.

Implementing MBWA within the chain of command requires a great deal of common sense. For example, given three levels of management in a division or department, it is quite appropriate for third-level managers to solicit information from first-level managers, and the second-level managers should not feel that they are being bypassed. Only on rare occasions, however, should the third-level managers give instructions and job assignments to first-level managers directly. When this type of action is called for, the third-level manager should immediately inform the second-level manager what has transpired. If managers would follow these simple common-sense guidelines, MBWA should not disrupt the normal chain of command.

In sum, the central message here is that you should view the management information system and managing by walking around as two mutually compatible means of gauging the progress of your work unit. The MIS will provide you with some useful "maps," but MBWA will provide you with immediate comprehension of what is going on in the "territory." You need to stay abreast of both the maps and the territory and, in addition, make certain that the maps are an accurate reflection of the territory.

COORDINATED PROBLEM SOLVING

A problem is said to exist whenever there is a discrepancy between a desired state and an actual state. At a given point in time, you had planned for your work unit to be at state A, but it is only at state B. Because there is a discrepancy between where you had planned to be and where you actually are, you no doubt realize that you have a problem.

Your measurement strategy inevitably will point up problems. It will identify discrepancies between the actual and the desired. How will you deal with these problems?

In terms of our leadership model, we can see four different approaches to dealing with problems:

1. The **Victim** will sit on the sidelines and blame the system for the problems.
2. The **Dreamer** will reflect on numerous solutions to the problems but will be unable to implement any of the solutions.
3. The **Doer** will attempt to solve the problems single-handedly.
4. The **Leader-Manager** will use coordinated problem solving in dealing with the problems.

Coordinated problem solving means involving all of the key players in solving a given problem. Here there are two questions: Who has a stake in seeing that the problem is solved? and Who can make a significant contribution to solving the problem? Perhaps the only people who should be involved are those in your own department. Or, perhaps there should be a mixture of people from your own department and people from one or more other departments. Perhaps it is important to get your manager involved. Whatever the situation, the guiding principle is to involve the *key players*.

The first step in the process is to define the problem clearly. As one writer has stated, "A problem clearly defined is half-solved." And be sure that you have defined the actual problem rather than a symptom of the problem.

Once the problem is clearly defined, involve the key players. Involve those people who have a vital interest in seeing the problem solved plus others who could serve in a consultative role.

With these interested parties involved in a problem-solving meeting, you should serve in a leadership role in taking the group through a systematic problem-solving process. The outcome of this meeting should be a plan of action for solving the problem.

Then implement the plan of action. And be sure to follow up. Be mindful that "a problem is not solved until it is solved."

This coordinated approach to solving problems will not guarantee success in solving every problem, but it will surely be more effective than that which is used by the Victim, the Dreamer, or the Doer. We cannot guarantee perfection, but we can promise an improvement in batting average.

PROBLEMS ARE THE REASON FOR MY JOB is the message on a sign that I once saw in a manager's office. This is what it is all about. If there were no problems, there would be no need for you in your present job. Day in and day out, as you endeavor to move from where you are toward your vision, you will be faced with problems. Accept this truism not as a cynical foreboding but as a way of life. And don't be a Victim. Rather, view yourself as a professional problem solver.

* * * * *

As we close this chapter on measuring, I would like to leave with you this thought:

> High tech without high touch is sterile;
> High touch without high tech is blind;
> But the uniting of high tech and high touch
>   will help you gauge your progress
>   as you advance toward your vision.

WHAT SHOULD BE DONE

I stated at the outset that leadership can be learned. This I believe. The key is to focus on *the functions of leadership.*

Being confident that you desire to become a more effective leader-manager, I suggest the following plan of action:

1. Evaluate yourself on the Leadership Assessment Inventory (Appendix A).

2. Work through the Case Study (Appendix B).

3. Complete the Personal Action Plan (Appendix C).

4. Review the Personal Action Plan with your manager.

5. Implement the Personal Action Plan.

Throughout this endeavor, periodically review the "Ten Commandments for Leader-Managers" presented on the following page. Reflect on these Ten Commandments until they become internalized in your self-being—*they become part of you.*

TEN COMMANDMENTS FOR LEADER-MANAGERS

I.   Make a commitment to being an effective leader.

II. Establish a climate for change that will lead to higher levels of achievement.

III. Formulate a clearly articulated vision of the future.

IV. Build a team of people who are jointly responsible for achieving the vision.

V.   Communicate the organizational values through your words and actions.

VI. Develop a strategy that will help you achieve the vision.

VII. Create a climate for authentic dialogue.

VIII. Motivate others by helping them move toward their ideal selves.

IX. Take a personal interest in the development of each of your people.

X.   Gauge progress on the basis of critical success factors.

Appendix A

Leadership Assessment Inventory

INSTRUCTIONS

This Assessment Inventory presents a comprehensive view of the effective leader. The ideas underlying the 100 items are drawn from the vast literature on leadership. Presented here is a model of the *ideal leader* — as viewed by experts in the field of leadership.

The purpose of the inventory is to help make a performance assessment of a manager *as a leader*. The assessment may be done in any of three ways: (1) the manager may evaluate himself or herself; (2) the manager's immediate supervisor may evaluate the manager; or (3) the people reporting directly to the manager may evaluate the manager. To obtain a comprehensive view of your own performance as a leader, you may want to use all three approaches.

The inventory includes ten items in each of ten areas: (1) Personal Attributes, (2) The Leader as Change Agent, (3) Creating the Vision, (4) Developing the Team, (5) Clarifying the Values, (6) Positioning, (7) Communicating, (8) Empowering, (9) Coaching, and (10) Measuring.

Read each statement carefully. Then respond to each item with a number from "0" through "5" according to the following scale:

5 = To a very large extent   2 = To a slight extent
4 = To a fairly large extent   1 = To a very slight extent
3 = To a moderate extent   0 = Not at all

After you have completed the inventory, compute each of the 10 category scores and record the scores on the following page.

LEADERSHIP PROFILE

Record each category score with a point on the graph, and then connect the points with straight lines using a colored pencil or pen.

		0	5	10	15	20	25	30	35	40	45	50
(1)	PERSONAL ATTRIBUTES											
(2)	THE LEADER AS CHANGE AGENT											
(3)	CREATING THE VISION											
(4)	DEVELOPING THE TEAM											
(5)	CLARIFYING THE VALUES											
(6)	POSITIONING											
(7)	COMMUNICATING											
(8)	EMPOWERING											
(9)	COACHING											
(10)	MEASURING											

1. PERSONAL ATTRIBUTES

1.1   Accepts and enjoys the role of leader.   _____

1.2   Is a self-confident person.   _____

1.3   Is self-motivated and self-directing.   _____

1.4   Has a firm sense of purpose and commitment.   _____

1.5   Is action-oriented — has a strong drive to
      accomplish and achieve.   _____

1.6   Is guided by a clear set of values.   _____

1.7   Is willing "to stand up and be counted"— even
      with an unpopular view.   _____

1.8   Is a decisive person.   _____

1.9   Is a person of integrity.   _____

1.10 Is continually learning, developing, and
      expanding.   _____

                                      Sum of scores=   _____

2. THE LEADER AS CHANGE AGENT

2.1   Can envision a new reality and aid in its
      translation into concrete terms.   _____

2.2   Is able to abandon outmoded assumptions and
      to experiment with some alternative concepts.   _____

2.3   Is a person who can make things happen.   _____

2.4   Is able to shape and push an idea until it
      takes usable form.   _____

2.5   Is able to get enough power to mobilize peo-
      ple and resources to initiate and implement
      an innovation.   _____

2.6   Actively involves his or her people in planning
      for change.   _____

2.7   Generates an attitude that change is normal.   _____

2.8   Is able to gain acceptance of change with a
      minimum of resistance.   _____

2.9   Seeks out and accepts criticism of his or her
      ideas.   _____

2.10 Is able to create a *pocket of excellence* on his
      or her turf.   _____

                                    Sum of scores =   _____

3. CREATING THE VISION

3.1   Demonstrates a good grasp of what the
      organizational unit is and how it is faring.   _____

3.2   Demonstrates a good grasp of the goals and
      strategic plans of the larger organization.   _____

3.3   Demonstrates an ability to focus on the
      critical issues.   _____

3.4   Demonstrates an ability to think beyond the
      daily routine, to see a greater vision that ties
      day-to-day activites to future goals.   _____

3.5   Demonstrates the ability to set a new direc-
      tion for the organizational unit for which he
      or she is responsible.   _____

3.6   Identifies an overarching goal that captures
      the unique thrust of his or her unit and pro-
      vides common purpose.   _____

3.7   Is able to attain a clear and coherent mental
      picture of what the organizational unit can
      become.   _____

3.8   Is able to transfer his or her mental picture of
      what the organizational unit can become to
      the minds of all members of the team.   _____

3.9   Is able to obtain "ownership" of the vision on
      the part of all team members.   _____

3.10 Is able to concentrate the attention of
      everyone in the unit on the vision.   _____

                              Sum of scores =   _____

4. DEVELOPING THE TEAM

4.1   Is able to create a team of key staff members
      who are *jointly responsible* with the manager
      for the unit's success.   _____

4.2   Promotes team spirit while at the same time
      being supportive of the goals of the larger
      organization.   _____

4.3   Creates an environment that fosters trust
      among the team members.   _____

4.4   Actively involves the team members in the
      formulation of group goals and objectives.   _____

4.5   Achieves among all team members a commit-
      ment to the group goals.   _____

4.6   Actively involves team members in key deci-
      sions that influence their work.   _____

4.7   Seeks advice and counsel from the team
      members.   _____

4.8   Promotes honest, sincere feedback among all
      members of the team.   _____

4.9   Promotes a win-win approach to conflict
      resolution.   _____

4.10 Actively involves the team members in
      evaluating group performance and deciding
      upon corrective action.   _____

                                    Sum of scores =   _____

5. CLARIFYING THE VALUES

5.1   Serves as the focal point of the unit in
      translating organizational values into reality.   _____

5.2   Demonstrates a clear understanding of the
      organization's value system.   _____

5.3   Is able to articulate and breathe life into the
      organization's value system.   _____

5.4   Communicates the organization's values in
      terms of specific statements on specific issues.   _____

5.5   By communicating the organizational values,
      is able to provide employees with a "compass"
      and point them in the proper direction.   _____

5.6   Makes decisions and acts in accord with the
      organization's value system.   _____

5.7   Is faithful in adhering to the organization's
      value system.   _____

5.8   Demonstrates consistency in actions and
      words.   _____

5.9   Rewards staff on the basis of their adherence
      to the organization's value system.   _____

5.10 Is successful in translating the organization's
      values into a reality that is manifest in the
      staff's daily behavior.   _____

                                    Sum of scores =   _____

6. POSITIONING

6.1   Is able to provide a realistic bridge from the present to the future of the organizational unit.   _____

6.2   Has a good grasp of the external environment insofar as it relates to his or her group.   _____

6.3   Has a good grasp of the needs and demands of clients.   _____

6.4   Has a good grasp of the strengths and limitations of his or her organizational unit.   _____

6.5   Identifies and focuses on key thrust areas.   _____

6.6   Develops an annual written plan that integrates goals, action sequences, and resources.   _____

6.7   Involves his/her staff in the development of plans.   _____

6.8   Asks "what if" questions — develops contingency plans.   _____

6.9   Reviews plans periodically and makes adjustments as appropriate.   _____

6.10   Has a systematic abandonment policy — knows when to "fold" in a given area.   _____

Sum of scores =   _____

7. COMMUNICATING

7.1 Is able to communicate in the language of the receiver. _____

7.2 Is a good listener. _____

7.3 Gives effective oral presentations. _____

7.4 Conducts effective and efficient meetings. _____

7.5 Is a good writer. _____

7.6 Lets staff know where the organization is headed, how it plans to get there, and what all that means to them. _____

7.7 Makes his or her *position on key issues* known to staff. _____

7.8 Provides his or her staff with accurate and complete information. _____

7.9 Manages by "walking around"– to engage in one-on-one dialogue with staff. _____

7.10 "Walks the talk"– actions are consistent with words. _____

Sum of scores = _____

8. EMPOWERING

8.1   Treats people as his or her most important
      asset.   _____

8.2   Treats people with dignity and respect.   _____

8.3   Shows true concern for each staff member as
      a person.   _____

8.4   Is able to perceive the needs of his or her
      people.   _____

8.5   Is effective in linking the needs of the in-
      dividual staff members and the needs of the
      organization.   _____

8.6   Demonstrates a clear commitment to
      excellence.   _____

8.7   Is able to attract and energize people to an
      exciting vision of the future.   _____

8.8   Motivates others through enthusiasm and in-
      fectious optimism.   _____

8.9   Is able to bring out the best in people—lifts
      them to their "higher selves."   _____

8.10 Is able to make his or her staff feel that they
      are winners.   _____

                              Sum of scores =   _____

9. COACHING

9.1 Cares enough about people to take the time to build a personal relationship with them. _____

9.2 Takes a personal interest in the career development of each member of his or her group. _____

9.3 Uses naturally arising interactions with staff to foster learning. _____

9.4 Makes effective use of work assignments as a major means of developing his or her staff. _____

9.5 Is an effective delegator. _____

9.6 Gives honest feedback in a timely fashion. _____

9.7 Uses performance appraisal as a means of teaching, not exhorting or admonishing. _____

9.8 Is effective in developing his or her followers to become leaders. _____

9.9 Is actively developing one or more backups for his or her position. _____

9.10 Promotes lifelong learning as "a way of life" for all members of the group. _____

Sum of scores = _____

10. MEASURING

10.1   Has a good grasp of the *nature of the system*
       for which he or she is responsible.   _____

10.2   Has a good grasp of the *state of the system* at
       any point in time.   _____

10.3   Has a good grasp of the relations between
       causal, intervening, and end-result variables
       in the system for which he or she is
       responsible.   _____

10.4   Is able to identify the "critical success fac-
       tors": the limited number of areas in which
       satisfactory results will ensure successful
       performance.   _____

10.5   Collects data and information continually on
       the critical success factors — those which are
       operationally most important.   _____

10.6   Maintains a balanced view in evaluating both
       the tangibles and the intangibles.   _____

10.7   Continually evaluates progress against plans.   _____

10.8   Conducts effective operations review meetings
       to evaluate overall performance.   _____

10.9   Deals with problems in proportion to their
       importance.   _____

10.10 Is effective in taking corrective action
       promptly whenever accomplishments deviate
       significantly from the plan.   _____

                                      Sum of scores =   _____

ACKNOWLEDGMENTS

The information for the items included in this inventory was obtained from the following sources:

Bennis and Nanus—*Leaders*
Bradford and Cohen—*Managing for Excellence*
Bullen and Rockart—*A Primer on Critical Success Factors*
Burns—*Leadership*
D'Aprix—*Communicating for Productivity*
Davis—*Managing Corporate Culture*
Deal and Kennedy—*Corporate Cultures*
Drucker—*The Effective Executive*
Dyer—*Team Building*
Gellerman—*Management by Motivation*
Iacocca—*Iacocca : An Autobiography*
Kanter—*The Change Masters*
Kilman—*Beyond the Quick Fix*
Koontz and O'Donnell—*Management*
Likert—*The Human Organization*
Maslow—*Eupsychian Management*
McGregor—*The Human Side of Enterprise*
Mintzberg—*The Nature of Managerial Work*
Pascale and Athos—*The Art of Japanese Management*
Peters and Waterman—*In Search of Excellence*
Peters and Austin—*A Passion for Excellenece*
Quinn—*Strategies for Change*
Ranftl—*R&D Productivity*
Sashkin—*A Manager's Guide to Participative Management*
Shea—*Building Trust in the Workplace*

Appendix B

A Case Study for Development of a Productive Department

THE PROBLEM

Department X in your organization is in rather serious trouble. Because of poor leadership over the past two years, the department has declined progressively in productivity, and the productivity of this department is *essential* to the present and future success of the organization as a whole. It is now apparent that a new leader must be brought in to head up the department and convert it into a viable operation.

During the past two years, three radically different leaders have headed up the department. First, there was Doer, who was a hard worker but had no vision of what the department might become. Next, there was Dreamer, who had a beautiful vision of what the department might become but was ineffectual in implementing the vision. Then, most recently, there was Victim, who sat on the sidelines and complained about lack of management support.

Upper management is well aware that they have been at fault in the selection of these three managers. Or, was it an education and training problem? Or perhaps a motivation problem? They really don't know. But what they do know is that they cannot afford to repeat the mistake once again. They are determined to select a winner.

The upper-level managers have studied the problem in depth and have arrived at these conclusions:

    1. Not one of the previous department managers was a *true leader.*

2. Not one of these managers was able to bring about *effective change*.
3. Similarly, the people have never had a clear picture of the *vision* — where the department is going.
4. The department has never had a *team spirit* — it has always been a collection of individuals going their separate ways.
5. The people in the department have never had a clear grasp of the organization's *values* — what the organization stands for and what is important to it.
6. As might be expected, the department has been lacking in *strategy* — insofar as having a roadmap for getting from A to B.
7. Perhaps the most telling deficiency in the group has been poor *communication* — upward, downward, and laterally.
8. As a result of all of the above, the present *motivation* level of the staff is very low.
9. Because the previous department managers placed so little emphasis on *developing others*, a backup for the manager was never developed from within — hence the need to go outside.
10. Finally, the previous department managers have done an inadequate job in *evaluating overall performance* — they never had a good grasp of what should be evaluated or how well the department was doing.

The results of this analysis have now prompted upper management to take immediate action in replacing Victim as department manager. They want a true leader, someone who can transform the department into a productive enterprise, one that will contribute substantially to the success of the total organization. They want someone who can turn the operation around and do it within the next 12 months. The situation is urgent.

On the basis of the preceding information, how would you respond to the questions on the following pages?

1. THE NATURE OF LEADERSHIP

Assuming that you are a member of upper management, what kind of person would you want to select to be the new manager of Department X?

a. Personal attributes:

b. Knowledge, skills, and experience:

2. THE LEADER AS CHANGE AGENT
(All of the remaining questions in this case study are addressed to you as the new department manager.)

Assume that you have been selected to be the new manager of Department X.

a. What would be your major sources of power for effecting change?

b. What would be your major barriers for effecting change?

c. How would you plan to deal with these barriers?

3. CREATING THE VISION

a. What would you include in a vision of the desired state of the department?

b. How would you go about creating the vision?

c. How would you obtain "ownership" of the vision on the part of all team members?

4. DEVELOPING THE TEAM

a. What actions would you take to build this collection of
   diverse personalities into a productive team?

b. What would you do to create a feeling of trust among all
   team members?

5. CLARIFYING THE VALUES

a. How would you go about identifying the principal values of
    the larger organization?

b. What actions would you take to translate the organizational
    values into practice?

6. POSITIONING

a. What would you include in a strategy for moving the department from its present state toward the vision?

b. How would you go about developing the strategy?

7. COMMUNICATING

a. What would be the most important types of information
   needed by the members of your department?

b. How would you go about communicating this information?

8. EMPOWERING

a. How would you go about assessing the motivation of your individual team members?

b. What methods of motivation do you believe would be most effective with the people in your department?

9. COACHING

a. What approach would you use to identify the developmental needs of your staff?

b. How would you go about meeting these developmental needs?

10. MEASURING

a. What would be the critical success factors associated with overall success of the department?

b. What data and information would you need to determine the status of each of these critical success factors?

Appendix C

Personal Action Plan

In the last analysis the individual must develop himself, and
he will do so optimally only in terms of what he sees as
meaningful and valuable. If he becomes an active party to
the decisions that are made about his development, he is
likely to make the most of the opportunities that are
presented.

Douglas McGregor
The Human Side of Enterprise, pp. 191–192

Completing the exercises on the following pages will help you become
a more effective leader. The final document should serve as a self-
development plan that you can apply in your position as leader-
manager. Please give deep thought to each question and then answer
each one on the basis of what you have learned to date and your
own judgment.

1. THE NATURE OF LEADERSHIP

Please complete the Leadership Assessment Inventory. After you have completed the Inventory, answer these two questions?

a. What are your major strengths as a leader?

b. In what areas do you need improvement?

2. THE LEADER AS CHANGE AGENT

a. What are the major sources of power that you have in your organization for effecting change?

b. What actions should you take for enhancing this power base?

3. CREATING THE VISION

a. What is the vision that you have for your group for the next three-year time period?

b. What actions will you need to take to convert the vision into reality?

4. DEVELOPING THE TEAM

a. What are the strengths and limitations of your present group with regard to its being a team of people working toward common goals?

b. What actions should you take to make your group a better team?

5. CLARIFYING THE VALUES

a. What are the principal values of the larger organization of
   which you are a part?

b. What actions should you take to translate these values into
   practice?

6. POSITIONING

a. What are the key features of your strategy for moving from where you now are toward your vision?

b. What will be the major obstacles in implementing the strategy?

c. How do you plan to overcome each of these obstacles?

7. COMMUNICATING

a. What are your strengths and limitations as a communicator?

Strengths   **Limitations**

b. What actions should you take to become a more effective communicator?

8. EMPOWERING

a. What are the primary motivators for each person who reports directly to you?

b. What actions should you take to better motivate these persons?

9. COACHING

a. What are the developmental needs of each person who
   reports directly to you?

b. What is one action you could take with each of these persons
   to help meet his or her developmental needs?

10. MEASURING

a. What are the critical success factors for your group during
   the coming year?

b. What data or information do you need to assess the status of
   each of these critical success factors?

c. How do you plan to obtain the data and information that
   you need?

Bibliography

Ackoff, Russell. *The Art of Problem Solving*. New York: John Wiley & Sons, 1978.

Anthony, Robert, and John Dearden. *Management Control Systems*. Homewood, Illinois: Richard D. Irwin, 1980.

Appley, Lawrence. *Formula for Success: A Core Concept in Management*. New York: American Management Associations, 1974.

Appley, Lawrence. *Management in Action: The Art of Getting Things Done Through People*. New York: American Management Associations, 1956.

Appley, Lawrence. *The Management Evolution*. New York: American Management Associations, 1963.

Appley, Lawrence. *Values in Management*. New York: American Management Associations, 1969.

Barnard, Chester. *Organization and Management*. Cambridge: Harvard University Press, 1948.

Bass, Bernard. "Leadership: Good, Better, Best." *Organizational Dynamics*, Winter 1985.

Behling, Orlando, and Charles Rauch, Jr. "A Functional Perspective on Improving Leadership Effectiveness." *Organizational Dynamics*, Spring 1985.

Benne, Kenneth, and Max Birnbaum. "Change Does Not Have To Be Haphazard." *The School Review*, LXIII, No. 3.

Bennis, Warren, and Burt Nanus. *Leaders: The Strategies for Taking Charge*. New York: Harper & Row, Publishers, 1985.

Blake, Robert, and Jane Mouton. "A Comparative Analysis of Situationalism and 9,9 Management by Principle." *Organizational Dynamics*, Spring 1982.

Block, Peter. *The Empowered Manager: Positive Political Skills at Work*. San Francisco: Jossey-Bass Publishers, 1987.

Bowers, David, and Jerome Franklin. "Survey-Guided Development: Using Human Resources Measurement in Organizational Change." *Journal of Contemporary Business*, Summer 1972.

Bradford, David, and Allan Cohen. *Managing For Excellence*. New York: John Wiley & Sons, Inc., 1984.

Buber, Martin. *Between Man and Man*. Boston: Beacon Press, 1955.

Buber, Martin. *Pointing the Way*. New York: Harper & Row, Publishers, 1957.

Bullen, Christine, and John Rockart. *A Primer on Critical Success Factors*. Cambridge, Massachusetts: Sloan School of Management, 1981.

Burns, James MacGregor. *Leadership*. New York: Harper & Row, Publishers, 1978.

Chase, Stuart. *Power of Words*. New York: Harcourt, Brace & World, 1954.

Christensen, C. Roland, et al. *Business Policy: Text and Cases*. Homewood, Illinois: Richard D. Irwin, 1978.

Colbert, Bertram. "The Management Information System." *Management Services*, Sept.–Oct. 1967.

D'Aprix, Roger. *Communicating for Productivity*. New York: Harper & Row, Publishers, 1982.

Davis, Stanley. *Managing Corporate Culture*. Cambridge, Massachusetts: Ballinger Publishing Company, 1984.

Deal, Terrence, and Allan Kennedy. *Corporate Cultures: The Rites and Rituals of Corporate Life*. Reading, Massachusetts: Addison-Wesley Publishing Company, 1982.

Dewey, John. *How We Think*. Boston: D. C. Heath and Company, 1933.

Drucker, Peter. *The Effective Executive*. New York: Harper & Row, Publishers (Harper Colophon Books), 1967.

Drucker, Peter. *Management: Tasks • Responsibilities • Practices*. New York. Harper & Row, Publishers, 1973.

Drucker, Peter. *Managing in Turbulent Times*. New York: Harper & Row, Publishers, 1980.

Dyer, William. *Contemporary Issues in Management and Organization Development*. Reading, Massachusetts: Addison-Wesley Publishing Company, 1983.

Dyer, William. *Strategies for Managing Change*. Reading,

Massachusetts: Addison-Wesley Publishing Company, 1984.

Dyer, William. *Team Building: Issues and Alternatives.* Reading, Massachusetts: Addison-Wesley Publishing Company, 1977.

Egerton, Henry, and James Brown. "Perspectives on Planning." *Planning and the Chief Executive*, The Conference Board, 1972.

Farson, Richard. "Praise Reappraised." *Harvard Business Review*, Sept.–Oct. 1963.

Follett, Mary Parker. *Freedom and Coordination.* London: Pitman, 1949.

Gellerman, Saul. *Management by Motivation.* New York: American Management Associations, 1968.

Gellerman, Saul. *Motivation and Productivity.* New York: American Management Associations, 1963.

Geneen, Harold. *Managing.* New York: Doubleday & Company, 1984.

Gerstner, Louis. "Can Strategic Planning Pay Off?" *Business Horizons*, Dec. 1972.

Giblan, Edward. "The Road to Managerial Wisdom — and How to Get on It." *Management Review*, April 1984.

Goethe, Johann Wolfgang. *Faust.* Baltimore, Maryland: Penguin Books, 1949. (first published in 1808).

Goetz, Billy. *Managerial Planning and Control: A Managerial Approach to Industrial Accounting.* New York: McGraw-Hill Book Company, 1949.

Guth, William, and Renato Tagiuri. "Personal Values and Corporate Strategy." *Harvard Business Review*, Sept.–Oct. 1965.

Hitt, William. *Management in Action.* Columbus, Ohio: Battelle Press, 1985.

Holmes, Robert. "Developing Better Management Information Systems." *Financial Executive*, July 1970.

Horton, Thomas. " What Works for Me": 16 CEOs Talk About Their Careers and Commitments. New York: Random House, Inc., 1986.

Human Synergistics. "Leader's Manual: Solving Problems and Planning for Change." Plymouth, Michigan, 1985.

Iacocca, Lee. *Iacocca: An Autobiography.* New York: Bantam Books, 1984.

Irwin, Patrick, and Frank Langham. "The Change Seekers." *Harvard Business Review*, Jan.–Feb. 1966.

Jaspers, Karl. "Philosophical Autobiography." In *The Philosophy of Karl Jaspers*, edited by Paul Arthur Schilpp. New York: Tudor Publishing Company, 1957.

Jowett, B. (Ed.). *The Dialogues of Plato*. New York: Random House, 1920.

Kant, Immanuel. *Groundwork of the Metaphysic of Morals*. New York: Harper & Row, Publishers, 1964.

Kanter, Rosabeth Moss. *The Change Masters*. New York: Simon and Schuster, 1983.

Katz, Daniel, and Robert Kahn. *The Social Psychology of Organizations*. New York: John Wiley & Sons, 1978.

Katz, Robert. "Toward a More Effective Enterprise." *Harvard Business Review*, Sept.–Oct. 1960.

Keidel, Robert. *Game Plans. Sports Strategies for Business*. New York: E. P. Dutton, 1985.

Kellogg, Marion. *Career Management*. New York: American Management Association, 1972.

Kepner, Charles, and Benjamin Tregoe. "Developing Decision Makers." *Harvard Business Review*, Sept.–Oct. 1960.

Kilman, Ralph. *Beyond the Quick Fix: Managing Five Tracks to Organizational Success*. San Francisco: Jossey-Bass Publishers, 1984.

Kilman, Ralph, Mary Saxton, and Roy Serpa. "Why Culture is Not Just a Fad." In *Gaining Control of the Corporate Culture*, edited by Kilman, Saxton, and Serpa. San Francisco: Jossey-Bass Publishers, 1985.

Koontz, Harold, Cyril O'Donnell, and Heinz Weihrich. *Management*. New York: McGraw-Hill Book Company, 1980.

Korzybski, Alfred. *Science and Sanity*. Lancaster, Pa.: Science Press Printing Company, 1933.

Landen, Delmar, and Howard Carlson. "New Strategies for Motivating Employees." In *The Failure of Success*, edited by Alfred Marrow. New York: American Management Associations, 1972.

Lawler, Edward. *Pay and Organization Development*. Reading, Mass.: Addison-Wesley Publishing Company, 1981.

Levinson, Harry. "Asinine Attitudes Toward Motivation." *Harvard Business Review*, Jan.–Feb. 1973.

Levinson, Harry. "Management by Whose Objectives?" *Harvard Business Review*, July–August 1970.

Likert, Rensis. *The Human Organization: Its Management and Value*. New York: McGraw-Hill Book Company, 1967.

Likert, Rensis. *New Patterns of Management.* New York: McGraw-Hill Book Company, 1961.

Lin, Yutang (ed.). *The Wisdom of Confucius.* New York: Random House (The Modern Library), 1938.

Lin, Yutang (ed.). *The Wisdom of Laotse.* New York: Random House (The Modern Library), 1948.

Lippitt, Gordon. *Organization Renewal: Achieving Viability in a Changing World.* New York: Meredith Corporation, 1969.

Livingston, Sterling. "Pygmalion in Management." *Harvard Business Review,* July–August 1969.

Lodge, George Cabot. "Business and the Changing Society." *Harvard Business Review,* March–April 1974.

Mace, Myles. "The President and Corporate Planning." *Harvard Business Review,* Jan.–Feb. 1965.

Machiavelli, Niccolo. *The Prince.* New York: The New American Library, 1980. (first published in 1532).

Maier, Norman. *The Appraisal Interview: Three Basic Approaches.* LaJolla, California: University Associates, 1976.

Maier, Norman. *Problem-Solving Discussions and Conferences: Leadership Methods and Skills.* New York: McGraw-Hill Book Company, 1963.

Markus, Hazel, and Paula Nurius. "Possible Selves." *American Psychologist,* Vol. 41, No. 9, Sept. 1986.

Maslow, Abraham. *Eupsychian Management.* Homewood, Illinois: Richard D. Irwin, 1965.

Maslow, Abraham. *Toward a Psychology of Being.* New York: Van-Nostrand Reinhold Company, 1968.

McConkey, Dale. *MBO for Nonprofit Organizations.* New York: AMACOM, a division of American Management Associations, 1975.

McGregor, Douglas. *The Human Side of Enterprise.* New York: McGraw-Hill Book Company, 1960.

McGregor, Douglas. *The Professional Manager.* New York: McGraw-Hill Book Company, 1967.

McMahon, John, and Joseph Yeager. "Manpower and Career Planning." In *Training and Development Handbook,* edited by Robert Craig. New York: McGraw-Hill Book Company, 1976.

Mead, Margaret. "The Future as the Basis for Establishing a Shared Culture." *Daedalus,* Vol. 94, No. 1.

Miller, J. G. "Information Input, Overload, and Psychopathology." American Journal of Psychopathology, 116, 1960.

Mintzberg, Henry. "The Manager's Job." *Harvard Business Review*, July–August 1975.

Mintzberg, Henry. *The Nature of Managerial Work*. Englewood Cliffs, New Jersey: Prentice-Hall, 1980.

Moustakas, Clark. *Loneliness and Love*. Englewood Cliffs, New Jersey: Prentice-Hall, Inc., 1972.

Naisbitt, John. *Megatrends*. New York: Warner Books, 1982.

Odiorne, George. *MBO II: A System of Managerial Leadership for the 80s*. Belmont, California: Fearon Pitman Publishers, Inc., 1979.

Ohmann, O. H. "Skyhooks." *Harvard Business Review*, May–June 1955.

Pascale, Richard, and Anthony Athos. *The Art of Japanese Management: Applications for American Executives*. New York: Simon and Schuster, 1981.

Paul, Ronald. "Battelle Values." *BMI Bulletin*, March 1982.

Peters, Thomas, and Robert Waterman. *In Search of Excellence: Lessons from America's Best-Run Companies*. New York: Harper & Row, Publishers, 1982.

Peters, Tom, and Nancy Austin. *A Passion for Excellence: The Leadership Difference*. New York: Random House, 1985.

Quinn, James Brian. *Strategies for Change: Logical Incrementalism*. Homewood, Illinois: Richard D. Irwin, 1980.

Ranftl, Robert. *R&D Productivity*. Los Angeles, California: Robert Matthew Ranftl, 1978.

Sashkin, Marshall. *A Manager's Guide to Participative Management*. New York: American Management Associations, 1982.

Schilpp, Paul Arthur, and Maurice Friedman (Eds.). *The Philosophy of Martin Buber*. LaSalle, Illinois: The Open Court Publishing Company, 1967.

Schuler, Randall. "Definition and Conceptualization of Stress in Organizations." *Organizational Behavior and Human Performance*, Dec. 1979.

Shartle, Carroll. *Executive Performance and Leadership*. London: Staples Press, 1957.

Shea, Gordon. *Building Trust in the Workplace*. New York: American Management Associations, 1984.

Sherwin, Douglas. "The Meaning of Control." *Dun's Review and Modern Industry*, Jan. 1956.

Strunk, William, and E. B. White. *The Elements of Style*. New York: Macmillan Publishing Company, 1979.

Swift, Marvin. "Clear Writing Means Clear Thinking Means . . ." *Harvard Business Review*, Jan.–Feb. 1973.

Tannenbaum, Robert, and Sheldon Davis. "Values, Man and Organizations." *Industrial Management Review*, Winter 1969.

Tannenbaum, Robert, Irving Weschler, and Fred Massarik. *Leadership and Organization: A Behavioral Science Approach*. New York: McGraw-Hill Book Company, 1961.

Thompson, Paul, Robin Baker, and Norman Smallwood. "Improving Professional Development by Applying the Four-Stage Career Model." *Organizational Dynamics*, Autumn 1986.

Tilles, Seymour. "How to Evaluate Corporate Strategy." *Harvard Business Review*, July–August 1963.

Timm, Paul. "The Way We Word." *Supervisory Management*, May 1978.

Williamson, John (Ed.). *The Leader-Manager*. New York: John Wiley & Sons, 1986.

Yankelovich, Daniel, and John Immerwahr. "Why the Work Ethic Isn't Working." New York: Public Agenda Foundation, 1983.

Zaleznik, Abraham. "Managers and Leaders: Are They Different?" *Harvard Business Review*, May–June 1977.

Zussman, Yale. "Learning from the Japanese: Management in a Resource-Scarce World." *Organizational Dynamics*, Winter 1983.

Author Index

Subject Index